WORLD CUP 2010 · GROUP

GROUP C

Sat Jun 12 (19.30)		Rustenburg
ENGLAND ☐	☐ USA	
Sun Jun 13 (12.30)		Polokwane
ALGERIA ☐	☐ SLOVENIA	
Fri Jun 18 (15.00)		Johannesburg EP
SLOVENIA ☐	☐ USA	
Fri Jun 18 (19.30)		Cape Town
ENGLAND ☐	☐ ALGERIA	
Wed Jun 23 (15.00)		Port Elizabeth
SLOVENIA ☐	☐ ENGLAND	
Wed Jun 23 (15.00)		Pretoria
USA ☐	☐ ALGERIA	

GROUP D

Sun Jun 13 (19.30)		Durban
GERMANY ☐	☐ AUSTRALIA	
Sun Jun 13 (15.00)		Pretoria
SERBIA ☐	☐ GHANA	
Fri Jun 18 (12.30)		Port Elizabeth
GERMANY ☐	☐ SERBIA	
Sat Jun 19 (15.00)		Rustenburg
GHANA ☐	☐ AUSTRALIA	
Wed Jun 23 (19.30)		Johannesburg SC
GHANA ☐	☐ GERMANY	
Wed Jun 23 (19.30)		Nelspruit
AUSTRALIA ☐	☐ SERBIA	

GROUP G

Tue Jun 15 (15.00)		Port Elizabeth
IVORY COAST ☐	☐ PORTUGAL	
Tue Jun 15 (19.30)		Johannesburg EP
BRAZIL ☐	☐ NORTH KOREA	
Sun Jun 20 (19.30)		Johannesburg SC
BRAZIL ☐	☐ IVORY COAST	
Mon Jun 21 (12.30)		Cape Town
PORTUGAL ☐	☐ NORTH KOREA	
Fri Jun 25 (15.00)		Durban
PORTUGAL ☐	☐ BRAZIL	
Fri Jun 25 (15.00)		Nelspruit
NORTH KOREA ☐	☐ IVORY COAST	

GROUP H

Wed Jun 16 (12.30)		Nelspruit
HONDURAS ☐	☐ CHILE	
Wed Jun 16 (15.00)		Durban
SPAIN ☐	☐ SWITZERLAND	
Mon Jun 21 (15.00)		Port Elizabeth
CHILE ☐	☐ SWITZERLAND	
Mon Jun 21 (19.30)		Johannesburg EP
SPAIN ☐	☐ HONDURAS	
Fri Jun 25 (19.30)		Pretoria
CHILE ☐	☐ SPAIN	
Fri Jun 25 (19.30)		Bloemfontein
SWITZERLAND ☐	☐ HONDURAS	

FOR KNOCKOUT STAGES, SEE BACK OF BOOK

THE BIG
BOOK OF THE
WORLD
CUP

BY
CLIVE BATTY AND
CIARAN CRONIN

Published by Vision Sports Publishing in 2010

Vision Sports Publishing
19-23 High Street
London
KT1 1LL

www.visionsp.co.uk

ISBN : 978-1905326-83-9

Editor: Jim Drewett
Authors: Clive Batty and Ciaran Cronin
Design: Neal Cobourne
Kit images: David Moor, www.historicalkits.co.uk
All pictures: Getty Images
Additional photography: Charlotte Trotman

Printed and bound in China by Toppan Printing Co Ltd

A CIP record for this book is available from the British library

CONTENTS

THE GREATEST SHOW ON EARTH

The best players and the finest teams playing the greatest game ever invented in some truly spectacular stadiums – the World Cup is quite simply the biggest and best sporting event on the planet. South Africa 2010 starts here!

This *Big Book of the World Cup* brings you the lowdown on all 32 teams at this, the first ever World Cup to be played in Africa. We've got a guide to all ten stadiums, an in-depth look at the superstars likely to light up the tournament, a complete day-by-day, match-by-match viewing guide as well as a brilliant scorechart to fill in as the tournament progresses. Plus there are a host of preview features and even a brief look at all the past World Cups. Roll on 11 June!

And what a World Cup it promises to be. Only two teams from the top 20 of FIFA's World Rankings – Croatia and Russia – have failed to qualify for this summer's tournament, meaning that the vast majority of the world's best players and biggest names will be on display in South Africa. You only have to have a quick look at Group G to see what an enticing prospect that is. On 15 June, Didier Drogba's Ivory Coast will take on

Cristiano Ronaldo's Portugal in Port Elizabeth, with both countries then going on to play Kaka's Brazil over the course of the next ten days. In terms of star quality, no group has so much talent packed into it.

English eyes, of course, will be firmly focused on Fabio Capello's side to see whether they really do have the skill, organization and determination to finally win the World Cup. With the tournament being played in a cool South African winter, could this possibly be a chance for the country that invented the game to win its biggest prize for the first time since 1966? Or will it be another summer of agony? Surely the nation will not have to go through another collective heartbreak in a dreaded penalty shoot-out.

After a relatively easy draw for the group stages, England will already have one eye on the quarter-finals where, with no major shocks in the games beforehand,

they would face France. In the other last eight matches, if the groups go to form, Argentina will play Germany, the Netherlands will take on Brazil and Italy will have the task of knocking-out Spain. Thank goodness FIFA have left a gap on the Sunday and Monday so everyone can draw breath. It could be the greatest weekend of football the World Cup has ever seen.

That's just one reason why the tournament will be the most commercially successful in the history of the World Cup. FIFA are expected to rake in a total of £2.1billion in 31 days, a sum that includes television rights across the world, ticket sales across the ten venues and the money earned from official sponsors who have coughed up millions to have their products associated with the 2010 World Cup. Each team playing in the tournament will earn a minimum of £5.2million, with the winners bringing home a cheque for £20million along with the World Cup trophy.

There will also be huge benefits for hosts South Africa. Three hundred and fifty thousand supporters will visit the country over the course of the tournament, with an estimated £175million expected to pour directly into the coffers of the tourism industry. More than 150,000 jobs will have been created in the construction and service industries by the time the tournament is over, and the whole country will benefit from the improvements made to South Africa's stadia and infrastructure.

But it's not really about the money – it's about the glory. A breathtaking goal will be remembered forever by the billions watching on television all over the world, as will a special flick or turn, while the members of the winning team will be feted in their native land until the day they die. A World Cup creates heroes and can define entire careers. It's all on the line in what's likely to be an unforgettable summer of football.

SIT BACK AND ENJOY

South Africa's match against Mexico at the Soccer City Stadium in Johannesburg on 11 June kicks-off a feast of football that will see 63 matches played in the space of 31 days at the 2010 World Cup. Thumb through the calendar and you'll find that over the course of the tournament there are only six days without any football to watch. Best of all, with South Africa just one hour behind, there will be no matches early in the morning or late at night for British viewers.

More good news is that all the games will be shown live on either BBC or ITV, with both channels sharing the fixtures out between them. The final, however, will be carried live on both channels. The BBC and ITV will also host nightly highlights programmes for those who are unable to sneak away from work to catch the action.

In total there will be more than 100 hours of live World Cup football to watch over the course of the tournament. On the opening day, Friday 11 June, there will be two live matches on offer but after that, and for the next ten days, viewers will have three live games a day to sink their teeth into. What a feast of football. After that, and until the end of the quarter-final stage, the schedule will revert back to two live games per day.

In all, a combined worldwide audience of 5.9 billion people will watch the 63 games – the 2008 Beijing Olympics posted a total of 4.7 billion viewers – with an expected 300 million expected to tune in for the final in Johannesburg on 11 July. The eyes of the world will truly be on the Soccer City Stadium that evening.

So, take the month off work, stock up the fridge, grab your favourite spot on the sofa, sit back and enjoy!

WORLD CUP VIEWING GUIDE

All kick-offs are in British Summer Time
(one hour behind South African time)

GROUP STAGE

FRIDAY 11 JUNE

3.00pm – **South Africa v Mexico**, Johannesburg,
Soccer City Stadium (Group A)

7.30pm – **Uruguay v France**, Cape Town (Group A)

SATURDAY 12 JUNE

12.30pm – **South Korea v Greece**, Port Elizabeth
(Group B)

3.00pm – **Argentina v Nigeria**, Ellis Park (Group B)

7.30pm – **England v USA**, Rustenburg (Group C)

SUNDAY 13 JUNE

12.30pm – **Algeria v Slovenia**, Polokwane (Group C)

3.00pm – **Serbia v Ghana**, Pretoria (Group D)

7.30pm – **Germany v Australia**, Durban (Group D)

MONDAY 14 JUNE

12.30pm – **Netherlands v Denmark**, Johannesburg,
Soccer City Stadium (Group E)

3.00pm – **Japan v Cameroon**, Bloemfontein (Group E)

7.30pm – **Italy v Paraguay**, Cape Town (Group F)

TUESDAY 15 JUNE

12.30pm – **New Zealand v Slovakia**, Rustenburg
(Group F)

3.00pm – **Ivory Coast v Portugal**, Port Elizabeth
(Group G)

7.30pm – **Brazil v North Korea**, Ellis Park (Group G)

WEDNESDAY 16 JUNE

12.30pm – **Honduras v Chile**, Nelspruit (Group H)

3.00pm – **Spain v Switzerland**, Durban (Group H)

7.30pm – **South Africa v Uruguay**, Pretoria (Group A)

THURSDAY 17 JUNE

12.30pm – **Argentina v South Korea**, Johannesburg,
Soccer City Stadium (Group B)

3.00pm – **Greece v Nigeria**, Bloemfontein (Group B)

7.30pm – **France v Mexico**, Polokwane (Group A)

FRIDAY 18 JUNE

12.30pm – **Germany v Serbia**, Port Elizabeth (Group D)

3.00pm – **Slovenia v USA**, Ellis Park (Group C)

7.30pm – **England v Algeria**, Cape Town (Group C)

Carlos Tevez and Argentina open their campaign against Nigeria on June 11

SATURDAY 19 JUNE

12.30pm – **Netherlands v Japan**, Durban (Group E)

3.00pm – **Ghana v Australia**, Rustenburg
(Group D)

7.30pm – **Cameroon v Denmark**, Pretoria (Group E)

SUNDAY 20 JUNE

12.30pm – **Slovakia v Paraguay**, Bloemfontein
(Group F)

3.00pm – **Italy v New Zealand**, Nelspruit (Group F)

7.30pm – **Brazil v Ivory Coast**, Johannesburg, Soccer
City Stadium (Group G)

MATCH CALENDAR

MONDAY 21 JUNE

12.30pm – **Portugal v North Korea**, Cape Town (Group G)

3.00pm – **Chile v Switzerland**, Port Elizabeth (Group H)

7.30pm – **Spain v Honduras**, Ellis Park (Group H)

TUESDAY 22 JUNE

3.00pm – **France v South Africa**, Bloemfontein (Group A)

3.00pm – **Mexico v Uruguay**, Rustenburg (Group A)

Aaron Lennon will be hoping to be in an England team that makes it to the second round

7.30pm – **Greece v Argentina**, Polokwane (Group B)

7.30pm – **Nigeria v South Korea**, Durban (Group B)

WEDNESDAY 23 JUNE

3.00pm – **Slovenia v England**, Port Elizabeth (Group C)

3.00pm – **USA v Algeria**, Pretoria (Group C)

7.30pm – **Australia v Serbia**, Nelspruit (Group D)

7.30pm – **Ghana v Germany**, Johannesburg, Soccer City Stadium (Group D)

THURSDAY 24 JUNE

3.00pm – **Paraguay v New Zealand**, Polokwane (Group F)

3.00pm – **Slovakia v Italy**, Ellis Park (Group F)

7.30pm – **Cameroon v Netherlands**, Cape Town (Group E)

7.30pm – **Denmark v Japan**, Rustenburg (Group E)

FRIDAY 25 JUNE

3.00pm – **Portugal v Brazil**, Durban (Group G)

3.00pm – **North Korea v Ivory Coast**, Nelspruit (Group G)

7.30pm – **Switzerland v Honduras**, Bloemfontein (Group H)

7.30pm – **Chile v Spain**, Pretoria (Group H)

SECOND ROUND

SATURDAY 26 JUNE

A 3.00pm – **Winner Group A v Runner up Group B**, Port Elizabeth

C 7.30pm – **Winner Group C v Runner up Group D**, Rustenburg

SUNDAY 27 JUNE

D 3.00pm – **Winner Group D v Runner up Group C**, Bloemfontein

B 7.30pm – **Winner Group B v Runner up Group A**, Johannesburg, Soccer City Stadium

MONDAY 28 JUNE

E 3.00pm – **Winner Group E v Runner up Group F**, Durban

G 7.30pm – **Winner Group G v Runner up Group H**, Ellis Park

TUESDAY 29 JUNE

F 3.00pm – **Winner Group F v Runner up E**, Pretoria

H 7.30pm – **Winner Group H v Runner up G**, Cape Town

QUARTER-FINALS

FRIDAY 2 JULY

QF 1 3.00pm – **Winner Match E v Winner Match G**, Port Elizabeth

QF 2 7.30pm – **Winner Match A v Winner Match C**, Johannesburg, Soccer City Stadium

SATURDAY 3 JULY

QF 3 3.00pm – **Winner Match B v Winner Match D**, Cape Town

QF 4 7.30pm – **Winner Match F v Winner Match H**, Ellis Park

SEMI-FINALS

TUESDAY 6 JULY

7.30pm – **Winner QF1 v Winner QF3**, Cape Town

WEDNESDAY 7 JULY

7.30pm – **Winner QF2 v Winner QF4**, Durban

3RD/4TH PLACE PLAY-OFF

SATURDAY 10 JULY

7.30pm – Port Elizabeth

WORLD CUP FINAL

SUNDAY 11 JULY

7.30pm – Johannesburg, Soccer City Stadium

Will David Beckham and Wayne Rooney be celebrating on July 11th?

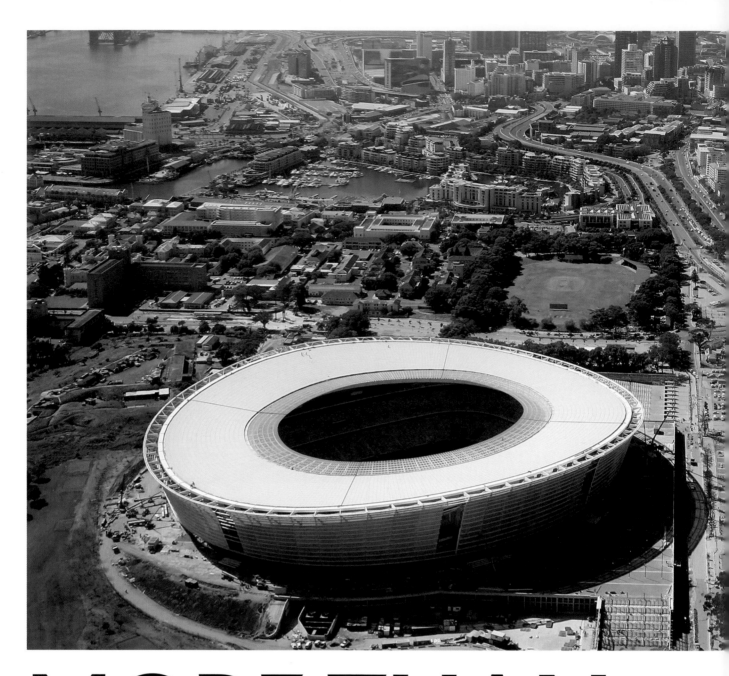

MORE THAN A GAME

For many South Africans football is symbolic of the struggle for freedom, so the hosting of the World Cup is a momentous landmark in the history of a nation striving to forge a new identity

The 19th World Cup will be played in front of one of the most beautiful backdrops imaginable. With 1,500 miles of picturesque coastline, countless safari parks and a whole host of vibrant and interesting cities, South Africa is a breathtaking country but one with a troubled political and social past. In 1948 a system of apartheid – a word meaning seperateness in the white South African language of Afrikaans – was brought into law by the all-white government and although the system was abolished when Nelson Mandela and his ANC party won power in the 1994 elections, the after-effects still linger around the country.

Any World Cup visitor arriving into Cape Town airport, for example, will have to drive past a vast shanty-town of corrugated iron roofs that is home to more than 20,000 people on their way to the city

Green Point Stadium in Cape Town is just one of the spectacular new stadiums built for the World Cup

centre. The country currently has an unemployment rate of close to 25 per cent and this has given rise to other social problems. A recent United Nations survey highlighted the fact that South Africa is the world's number one country for assaults, and number two in the world for murder.

Yet despite the problems the country is faced with, there remains a joy surrounding this World Cup because of the place football has in the hearts of the majority of the country's population. Rugby and cricket have always been the sports that South Africa has been most famous for on the international stage but the country's black population, which makes up 79

per cent of the total of 49 million, devote themselves almost entirely to the beautiful game. Down the years it has always proved an escape from the many problems the country has faced. The 1995 Rugby World Cup win and the iconic moment when Nelson Mandela handed over the William Webb Ellis Cup to Springbok rugby captain Francois Pienaar may have sparked wild celebrations in the country but they would be nothing compared to what would happen if the captain of Bafana Bafana (the nickname for the South African football team meaning 'the Boys, the Boys') was to get his hands on the World Cup trophy on 11 July in Johannesburg.

Left: Nelson Mandela presents the Rugby World Cup to Francois Pienaar

Right: South Africa's passionate support, black and white fans together

During the days of apartheid football became symbolic of the fight for freedom in South Africa. At the famous Robben Island prison off the coast of Cape Town, political

The renovated Soccer City Stadium in Johannesburg - the most iconic World Cup venue

prisoners imprisoned for their opposition to the apartheid movement, who included Nelson Mandela, fought for the right to play football. The detainees were allowed few privileges while in custody but in 1965, after much campaigning, they were eventually given permission to set up their own football competition on the island. The Makana FA, as the organising committee of the league called themselves, were given official recognition by FIFA and competitive football on the island became the main source of entertainment and diversion. Nine clubs were formed, with each putting out three different teams, and inmates who were not playing – a number which included Mandela – would peer out of their cells to watch the action.

Matthew Booth - a lone white figure in most Bafana Bafana team line-ups

"The league presented the triumph of the human spirit," said Tokyo Sexwale, a member of FIFA's fair play committee who was once a prisoner on the island. "What kept us together? Loneliness from home, from our children, from our wives, fathers and mothers. We came here young, with our feet and eager to play sport. We were not allowed to play any indoor or outdoor games but in the end the spirit of survival prevailed."

Lizo Sitito, another former inmate on Robben Island, also stressed how important the sport became to the men incarcerated in their cells for up to 22 hours a day. "Football saved my life," he said. "A person locked up and doing nothing cannot think. When soccer was there it gave us something to talk up about. That's why it's more than just a game."

The arrival of the World Cup will also be a landmark

in the development of the new South Africa because of the country's long-time expulsion from the international game. FIFA threw the Football Association of South Africa (FASA) out of their organisation in 1964 because they refused to select a racially mixed team – the laws of the country meant that they could either send an all white or an all black team – and South Africa weren't re-admitted to world football's family until the age of apartheid began to draw to a close in 1992 and the South African Football Association (SAFA) was formed. Since then, they have participated in the 1998 and 2002 World Cups although without much success.

Indeed, this lengthly absence from the international game has had an interesting knock-on effect which will make for an added ingredient to the atmosphere at this summer's tournament. For while the locals in South Africa will undoubtedly be going football mad this summer, many of them will be more interested in watching the other nations in action rather than their own. After years of being on the outside, the country's football fans have become used to cheering on other countries and they have been pretty slow to change. When England played a friendly against Bafana Bafana in May 2003 there were more native supporters cheering for Sven Goran Eriksson's team at King's Park in Durban than for the home team. Indeed, tickets for this summer's World Cup matches involving England, Brazil, Holland, Argentina and Italy have sold faster than the games involving Carlos Alberto Parreira's side.

"You cannot believe that other countries, from a ticketing point of view, are more popular than Bafana in our own country," says Danny Jordaan, the 2010 World Cup organising committee's chief executive. "It is a strange thing. In Germany in 2006 all the tickets for the German team were sold out first. But things seem to be a bit different here."

Old habits would seem to die hard and another effect from the apartheid era can been seen in the racial make-up of the Bafana Bafana side that will play at the World Cup. Only one white player, centre-half Matthew Booth, is likely to feature for the hosts for two simple reasons. Firstly, not a lot of white children play the game growing up, preferring rugby and cricket instead

The match balls await the arrival of the giants of world football

and secondly, few white children were allowed to mix with black youngsters on the football pitch during the apartheid era so they fell behind in their development. Booth seems to be the exception to both rules.

"We only played rugby and cricket at my all-white boys school and those sports were almost pushed down your throat," he explains. "To play football I had to go to a local club after school. It had an open-door policy allowing blacks and whites to play together, which was probably against the law at that time. It meant that from the age of five I was playing alongside black and coloured kids, when my schoolmates would never have come into contact with them. I was lucky that my dad encouraged me to play football, because he loved playing the game as a kid."

When Booth was playing alongside black kids in the early 1980s, football was most definitely the game of the townships and had been for a number of decades. One of the main attractions of the game has always been its simplicity and in the makeshift towns that sprung up around South Africa's major cities from the 1940s onwards, the game flourished as participants made their own balls out of newspapers and constructed their goalposts out of whatever materials they could get their hands on. In a time of little money, it was a cheap form of entertainment. Around that time the domestic league also began to flourish, particularly as South African football fans had no international team to support from the 1960s to 1990s. Huge crowds would gather to watch teams like the Kaiser Chiefs and the Orlando Pirates, the two most popular teams in the country who both hail from the Soweto district of Johannesburg, play in the National Professional Soccer League, which was formed in 1971.

Today the league's successor, the ABSA Premiership, is not nearly as popular among South African football fans. The Kaizer Chiefs attract crowds of about 20,000 to every home game but a number of the 16 teams in the top division fail to attract more than 3,000 spectators through their gates. Jordaan, the organising committee's chief executive, blames the increased access many South Africans have to English, Spanish and Italian football on television. They watch all that quality football from abroad and find it difficult to get excited about shelling out their hard-earned cash to watch teams that are not even half as good as Europe's finest. But Jordaan believes that the formation of an African Champions League in the next few years could change the domestic game forever. There is also some hope that the World Cup will encourage the country's football loving fans to get back

supporting their local professional teams, particularly the sections of the white population who love the sport.

"At the moment the white population are armchair supporters," explained Irvin Khoza, chairman of the

The World Cup organisers are hoping that all of South Africa will get behind their team in the tournament

league. "They don't come to the stadium. But during the Confederations Cup we had a big transformation. We had 50 per cent white and 50 per cent black. It was a big transformation. We hope to improve on that going forward. It is not enough for them to be watching at home, they must be at the stadium."

If that happens, then maybe football can truly unite the whole South African nation and finish off the work that the Rugby World Cup winning team of 1995 started.

FORZA ENGLAND!

With his strict, no-nonsense regime Fabio Capello has transformed England from a shambles to serious World Cup contenders. Could this be the year?

What a difference a couple of years can make. After England's defeat to Croatia at Wembley in November 2007, the entire nation was depressed at the thought of England's absence from Euro 2008. Two and a half years down the line there's a buzz of expectation surrounding the country's participation at this summer's World Cup.

That expectation was heightened in December when the World Cup draw was made in Cape Town. Algeria, Slovenia and the USA aren't exactly the most feared nations in world football and coupled with England's impressive record of nine wins out of ten games in the

qualifying campaign – the only defeat coming to the Ukraine when they were already assured of their place at the finals – there's a real expectation that John Terry and his men can go to South Africa this summer and take on the world.

Of course, we've heard all this kind of talk before but with Fabio Capello in charge, there's a genuine confidence that things might be different. The 63-year-old, who has managed the likes of Real Madrid, AC Milan, Roma and Juventus throughout his illustrious career in the dugout, has delivered success wherever he has been. When the going gets tough in big games, Capello knows how to get his players going.

He has proved that during England's stroll through the qualifying process but in the early days of his reign, Capello was on the end of some heavy critcism, like many England mangers have been before him. "That was one of the worst performances I have seen from an England team," said Harry Redknapp after England's 2-2 draw in a friendly against the Czech Republic in August 2008. "What positives can you take from that? The second half was diabolical. They didn't look like the same players who perform week in, week out in the Premier League. What are we doing to them?" But since then, Capello has changed people's views – Redknapp included – about his ability to relate to England's players and he has impressed everybody with the simple rules which have seemingly changed attitudes in the international squad.

Players have been banned from using mobile phones everywhere except in their own rooms - when Emile

Top: Steven Gerrard has finally found his role for England

Above: David Beckham could well have a key role to play from the bench

FORZA ENGLAND

Left: Frank Lampard has been re-born under Capello

Below: Wayne Rooney has impressed playing off Emile Heskey

Heskey was caught texting at the dinner table, Capello made an example of him in front of the rest of the squad. Speaking of dinner, all the team must eat together at an appointed time and room service has been banned. No visitors are allowed in the team hotel at any time and all players have to be in their own rooms by 10pm. Use of Playstations and other games consoles is allowed, but not encouraged. "Because we don't have long to work together compared to working at clubs, we need strict rules," explains Capello. "If we follow those rules, we'll create a group and a specific winning mentality, which is what I and the players want."

Another new departure in the Capello era has been the Italian's decision to reveal his team to the players just three hours before kick-off. "Ten minutes before we left for Wembley on the bus, he [Capello] had a flip chart and lifted up a sheet of paper to reveal one with the team on it," said David James after Capello's first game in charge. "Nobody had a clue. I think that's best, rather than having the 11 chosen the day before and giving everyone else the opportunity not to focus."

Overall, England's players seem to have welcomed Capello's way of going about business. "Capello was exactly what we needed," says Frank Lampard, who has been a regular under the Italian. "We needed a bit more selflessness in the side. At times it was easy to see we played as individuals too much in the past. We have very, very good individuals, but the team didn't perform because we weren't playing as a group. To play as a team, you need to have humility and to be selfless. You need to work for your mate next to you, or to play out of position if that's what is required. That kind of thing. That's something he needed to bring, and he's brought it."

Lampard also feels that his boss has dealt with the pressures surrounding his job in a positive way. "Everyone has an opinion on England – quite rightly so because we're all English – but we need a strong man who will not listen to anyone else and will go his route," the Chelsea midfielder points out. "The England job is the hardest for me because of that intense pressure, the fact that you're not able to work with your players regularly, and that everyone has an opinion as to who should be playing. It takes a strong man with a strong mind [to succeed in the role]."

Off the pitch, then, Capello would seem to have

emphasis on their defence, they are compact and well-organised, they move the ball on quickly, they are strong in the air and they are a real threat from dead balls, with players who can deliver superbly."

The true test, of course, will come in June and July. As is his nature, Capello is cautious about England's group draw and what it means for their chances of winning the tournament. "I have always said that if we want to arrive in the finals, we have to beat all the teams," he said. "The USA, Algeria and Slovenia are just the first three teams and it will not be easy because every team you play in World Cup is different because of the pressure. I respect the USA and I saw the way they played against Spain in the Confederations Cup. They will know what they have to do. We respect all the teams but we will play every game without fear."

England's captain John Terry has also preached a similar message of no-fear and he feels the squad simply have to deliver.

it all figured out and he's worked a trick or two on the pitch, too. The age-old question about whether Lampard and Steven Gerrard can play together on the same pitch hasn't been up for discussion these past 12 months because Capello has proven that they can. Il Capo has generally placed Lampard alongside Gareth Barry in central midfield, with Gerrard taking up a position drifting in from wide left, but both players have interchanged positions over the course of games and appear pretty comfortable in their new roles.

As does Wayne Rooney, who has been asked to play deep behind a big, physical striker, which more often than not has been Emile Heskey. It is a role that that appears to get the best from Rooney's incredible array of talents and with Gerrard drifting in to support him from the left, and a flier like Aaron Lennon or Theo Walcott on the right wing, there's little doubt that Capello's England possess plenty of attacking options. That said, it is the overall organisation of the England side that has impressed other international managers. "You can really see the impact that Capello has made," says Spain manager Vicente Del Bosque. "He has made England into England once again. He has placed great

"We've been labeled the 'Golden Generation' and soon we'll find out if we can live up to the billing," he says. "For myself, Frank Lampard, Steven Gerrard, David James, Ashley Cole and Rio Ferdinand it's now or never. If we don't do ourselves justice or do ourselves proud, this could be it. The opening game against the USA will be critical. They have proved they can play against the best in the world. The boss has drummed into us the need to be professional and to respect our opponents and keep our feet on the ground."

If Capello has been preaching such virtues to his squad, it's easy to understand why. As a player, he went to the 1974 World Cup in Germany with an Italian team that were among the favourites to win the trophy. They were pitted against Argentina, Poland and Haiti in what was considered a manageable group but the Azzurri failed to finish in the top two and departed home before the real business got underway. That's the kind of thing that can happen at a World Cup. Capello has had his fingers burnt before but will hope that his painstaking preparations with England will be enough to stop that happening on his second trip to the World Cup finals.

CAPELLO IN QUOTES

"Forget about everything else. You are here to work. You train, eat and rest. I don't want you doing anything else."

Capello's opening address to England's players.

"When you come to the England squad, you soon discover you have to be punctual. Fabio doesn't stand for lateness and will embarrass you in front of your teammates if you're not on time for something. I got a taste of that on my first trip to Spain last season. I'm not saying exactly what happened but I learned my lesson."

Carlton Cole on why you should never cross the Italian.

"We needed a very strong man in charge. Sure, in terms of the off-the-field stuff he's brought in – the discipline around the place in terms of dress, around the hotel, or dinners – but also in footballing terms. We needed a very strong leader who had his own mind. With Capello, we have that."

Frank Lampard outlines his admiration for England's manager.

"Sometimes he just walks by as if you're not even there and it can be quite intimidating. The way he holds himself, the way he looks at you. You just know he's a tough man - he has that aura about him."

Wayne Rooney on Capello.

"He doesn't treat any player in the team or in the squad any differently. He only makes decisions on football, he doesn't care about anything else. If he doesn't think you're fit, he won't play you; if he doesn't think you are good enough, he won't pick you."

David Beckham's view on the manager he once fell out with at Real Madrid.

"He has instilled a lot of confidence, belief and courage to play. Sometimes in the past we got a little bit scared of the ball, particularly at home, and we were scared to make a mistake. Now it's different. People will make mistakes but the manager has brought a lot out of the players."

Ashley Cole on the England manager.

"As you're watching, you know the minute you've made your mistake, or a misplaced pass, and you're thinking, 'Please don't stop it now'. Then he [Capello] stops it and gets his red beam and flashes it at you."

John Terry explains how Capello points out mistakes to England's players.

NO WAGS ZONE

This time it will be different. Whereas back in 2006 England's World Cup base in Baden Baden resembled a catwalk as the WAGs strolled around in designer clothes and jewellery in front of the world's media, on this occasion Fabio Capello will ensure his South African training camp is more like a monastery.

"When we are in South Africa, hopefully for a long

Top: The England training camp at the Royal Bafokeng Sports Palace

Above: There will not be much for the WAGS to do in the town centre!

period of time, the players will need the wives, the girls, the friends, but it will be one day a week, after each game," says the Italian. "That's enough. If they don't want to come for the day, they should stay at home. We are there to play, not for a holiday."

England will base themselves at the £20million Royal Bafokeng Sports Complex in Rustenburg, a facility just 30 minutes away from Pilanesberg International Airport and no more than a five minute drive to the Royal Bafokeng Sports Palace, where England will play their opening game in Group C against the USA. Crucially, it is also located 5,000 feet above sea level which makes it an ideal venue for the kind of altitude training that all teams in the tournament will need to undertake. The facility will be closed to the public and, as Capello has stated, the wives and girlfriends of the players will only be allowed visit for a brief period after each England game.

The England manager has even been involved in the design of the newly-built facility. He has already asked for two tennis courts to be moved as he wanted a clear view of the training pitches from the hotel. He has also asked for the grass on those pitches to be upgraded to the standard that England will play on when the World Cup gets underway. The medical facilities at the centre, however, as well as the gym and saunas are believed to be exactly to the Italian's liking.

All these excellent facilities will bear witness to an awful lot of hard work. After a mini-training camp at altitude in Irdning, Austria, a facility Capello has previously used with Real Madrid, England will arrive in Rustenburg in the last few days of May to continue their altitude training as they attempt to get their bodies used to the lower levels of oxygen in the air in the venues situated high above sea level.

That process will take anything up to ten days but at least England's players can relax in the lap of luxury once their day's work is over. The hotel attached to the sports complex will have 82 rooms, all of which will be equipped with extra long king-size beds, 32-inch plasma screens, double sinks in the bathroom and granite worktops. There's also a coffee shop on site, as well as two bars, which both boast custom-built wine cellars, something that should be to Capello's liking.

THE DREADED SPOT-KICKS

Fabio Capello has gone out of his way to avoid talking about penalty shoot-outs in the build up to the World Cup but let's hope he has some kind of plan up his sleeve in case any of England's games are decided by spot-kicks in South Africa. Put simply, England have the worst record of the top nations in world football when it comes to winning penalty shoot-outs, having won just one of the six in which they have participated. That success came in Euro '96 at Wembley against Spain but the five shoot-out failures – from Turin to Gelsenkirchen – will never be forgotten.

Penalty shoot-out record of top nations in major tournaments

Nation	Shoot-outs	Success Rate
Argentina	11	73%
Germany	7	71%
Brazil	11	64%
France	6	50%
Spain	7	42%
Italy	7	28%
Holland	5	20%
England	6	17%

Year	Stage	Opponents	Villains
1990	WC semi-final	W. Germany	Stuart Pearce Chris Waddle
1996	Euro semi-final	Germany	Gareth Southgate
1998	WC last 16	Argentina	Paul Ince David Batty
2004	Euro quarter-final	Portugal	David Beckham Darius Vassell
2006	WC quarter-final	Portugal	Frank Lampard Steve Gerrard Jamie Carragher

THE AFRICAN DREAM

No African team has ever got past the quarter-finals of the World Cup, but will South Africa 2010 – the first World Cup ever to be played in Africa – be the tournament when that changes? Could one of them even win it?

Many moons have now passed since Pele made his famous prediction that an African country would win the World Cup before the end of the century but with that deadline now well and truly passed, maybe the occasion of the first World Cup on African soil will inspire the teams of the continent to win football's greatest prize.

It won't be before time. No African team has ever made it past the quarter-finals of a World Cup despite a handful of sides from the continent lighting up a number of tournaments past. All but two of the previous 18 World Cups have been won by a country from the same continent as the hosts – Brazil winning the tournament in Sweden in 1958 and triumphing again in South Korea and Japan in 2002. There will be six African teams trying to ensure that

Emmanuel Eboue and co celebrate another Ivory Coast goal in qualifying

there is not another one by the conclusion of South Africa 2010.

And according to the countries themselves, the prospect of an African captain lifting the trophy at the Soccer City Stadium on 11 July is more than just a dream. "We have six good African teams in the World Cup - if they have good organisation and really good preparation there will be a big surprise from the African teams here," says Roger Milla, the former Cameroon striker whose swaying hips were a highlight of the 1990 World Cup. "Today football has become simple for everyone so even an

The Ivory Coast's most famous citizen is feted with a giant poster

Ghana celebrate victory in the 2009 Under 20 World Cup

African team has the ability to win the tournament. The proof is that Ghana won the recent U20 World Cup, while Nigeria reached the U17 final, so Africa can definitely contest the World Cup final itself. The African teams just need good preparation."

Former Nigeria captain Sunday Oliseh, who played in both the 1994 and 1998 World Cups for his country and also won Olympic gold at the Atlanta games in 1996, has expressed similar feelings. "The idea that one of our sides could win the World Cup is not going too far. African players perform a lot on emotions and that will be a powerful force. When Nigeria played at the Olympics in 1996 we were not playing as Nigerians but as Africans because we had every African country behind us. We had this psychological edge and if an African nation gets to the semi-finals on home soil in 2010, I would not want to be in the team who plays against them."

Oliseh makes a telling point. All of Africa's teams will be well supported at the tournament, not only because of the numbers that will travel from all over the continent to support their country in South Africa, but also because of the home support. Whereas in Europe you wouldn't expect a German crowd to get behind France in a game against Brazil, in South Africa this summer the local football fans will lend their full support to each and every one of their continental neighbours. Extensive violence may have broken out before and after the World Cup qualifying play-off game between Algeria and Egypt last November, but in South Africa this summer all of the continent's supporters will be united behind a common goal.

The Ivory Coast are one team that are going to need that kind of support from their African brothers. Didier Drogba and his teammates have been drawn in the 'Group of Death' alongside Brazil, Portugal and North Korea and a side that were tipped for great things before the draw now have a huge fight on their hands to even get out of their group. Still, on paper they represent the strongest of the African challengers with

a squad that includes Drogba, Arsenal's Emmanuel Eboue, former Tottenham midfielder Didier Zokora, Aruna Dindane of Portsmouth and Chelsea's Salomon Kalou. They are good players, one and all, and despite the level of difficulty of their group, the Ivory Coast can travel to South Africa in the knowledge that none of their opponents will be too keen on playing them either.

Ghana, the second best team on the continent according to FIFA's rankings, are in another tough group alongside Germany, Australia and Serbia. Chelsea's Michael Essien is their star performer but one major advantage they'll have is their experience from the 2006 World Cup in Germany. Ghana went to that tournament with the youngest squad of the 32 nations – the average age was 24 – and the vast majority of them are still around, older and wiser, for another go at it. "We are capable of winning the World Cup, we have a very formidable team with most of our boys playing in Europe," predicts Ghana FA President Kwesi Nyantakyi. "These are tried and tested players

who are able to face any kind of challenge anywhere. At the 2006 finals, Ghana could have gone further in the tournament [they lost in the second round to Brazil] but for a lack of experience, as well as confidence that we could do it. But, having gone through our first World Cup, I think we have enough experience now, which can push us very far and put us in contention for the ultimate title."

Cameroon and their fans are capable of making it through to the second round

They, like the Ivory Coast, are capable of getting out of their group, as are Nigeria and Cameroon. Nigeria didn't play all that well during qualifying but in Group B alongside Argentina, South Korea and Greece, the Super Eagles are well capable of doing enough to progress to the second round. The Everton pair of Joseph Yobo and Yakubu are Nigeria's key men and with Nwankwo Kanu of Portsmouth likely to be named in the squad, they won't lack for experience. Likewise Cameroon with Rigobert Song, the uncle of

THE AFRICAN DREAM

Above: South Africa will be up against it in Group A

Left: The Vuvuzela will act as a sound track to the World Cup

Arsenal midfielder Alex, who will be playing at his fourth World Cup at the age of 33. The Indomitable Lions will be in contention to finish in the top two of a group containing Holland, Japan and Denmark. Samuel Eto'o, their prolific striker, will be one of the most feared marksmen in the tournament and if he finds the net regularly, nobody will keen to meet them.

However, on paper the African challenge is not as strong when it comes to Algeria and South Africa. Algeria, the team from the north of the continent, have gone from 100th to 28th in the world rankings under the guidance of coach Rabah Saadane but they're still not considered a threat, something Fabio Capello and

England will sincerely hope. As for the host nation, the build-up to the finals has not been easy. Joel Santana, a manager who never had a job outside of Brazil before taking over South Africa, quit last October after Bafana Bafana lost eight of their previous nine matches and has been replaced by fellow Brazilian Carlos Alberto Parreira, who managed South Africa for one year back in 2007. Parreira doesn't lack experience – he has coached Kuwait, the UAE, Saudi Arabia and Brazil (twice) at previous World Cups, winning the tournament with his native land back in 1994 – but he's going to have a tough job moulding a largely domestic based side into a serious international outfit. And that's before other factors start to come into play.

While the Ivory Coast and Ghana could cause damage if they emerge from their tricky groups, and Nigeria and Cameroon will be extremely competitive whoever they face, the success of the African teams this summer could depend on how well they can manage other factors such as appearance money, training facilities and travel arrangements. Cameroon's players famously threatened to strike before their 1994 World Cup game against Brazil because they were owed two months wages by the country's FA. "There have always been problems off the pitch which prevent our teams from having that extra edge to go further," says Oliseh. "In 2002 it took Cameroon two days to get to their base; they were the last team to arrive in South Korea. There were so many administrative problems, with things like travelling, flights and player bonuses, that the players weren't focused enough."

There is no guarantee that situations like this won't occur in advance of this summer's World Cup, particularly as groups of players largely used to the professionalism of the game in Europe come up against administrators from their home countries who have no experience of how the modern game works.

But if there is one thing you can never accuse African footballers of it's not caring. Down the years they have taken part in countless bizarre rituals simply to ensure that the Gods are on their side. Take this tale from former Liverpool goalkeeper Bruce Grobbelaar, who made 32 international appearances for Zimbabwe. "We would stand around at the youth centre stripped naked desperately hoping none of the locals would see us. We would go into the witch doctor one at a time to have water swished over us with a goat's tail." From more recent times, Samuel Eto'o remembers seeing Nigeria standing in the tunnel outside their dressing-room before a game against Cameroon. "They said they weren't going in because we'd put a spell on their dressing room," he explained. Half of the Cameroon team then decided they didn't want to go into their dressing-room either and not one player from either side put on a shin-pad or pair of shorts until a local mystic arrived to purify both areas.

There are more stories. Philippe Troussier, who has managed the Ivory Coast, Nigeria, South Africa and Morocco in his career, tells a fascinating story of when he was in charge of the Ivory Coast on a trip to Algiers. "The second day I was there, I sat down for the team meal, and suddenly

African football can often work in mysterious ways

THE AFRICAN DREAM

Roger Milla shakes his hips at the 1990 World Cup

there were two men at the table I had never seen before in my life: two small people, like pygmies. I try to say 'no, no, no' in those sorts of situations but then they told me, 'OK, we need one pygmy for each player.' And then they came with a lady, and supposedly a virgin, a beautiful lady."

And of course they have their lucky charms, too. In the African Cup of Nations in 2000 a former President of the Nigerian FA ran onto the pitch and stole a charm that had been laid in the back of the Senegal net. Nigeria went on to score twice and win the game and the losers claimed it was all because of the goalmouth robbery.

But African football isn't all about rituals and superstitions. The teams know how to play, the continent's top players turn out for some of the best clubs in Europe – Samuel Eto'o at Inter Milan, Didier Drogba and Michael Essien at Chelsea – and

with passionate support behind them in every single game, there's no good reason why at least one of the six African countries can't make a major impact this summer.

AFRICAN TEAMS AT THE WORLD CUP

CAMEROON 1990

In the opening game of the 1990 World Cup, nobody gave Cameroon a prayer against holders Argentina but a header from Omam Biyick gave the African side a victory that made world football sit up and take notice. After that, a Roger Milla inspired Cameroon beat Romania 2-1 to qualify for the second round and they defeated Colombia 2-1 to set up a quarter-final showdown with England. When David Platt put England ahead early in the game it looked like the dream was over but quick-fire second-half goals from Emmanuel Kunde and Ebelle Ekeke put the Indomitable Lions on the brink of the semi-finals. However, a Gary Lineker penalty sent the game into extra time and England killed the fairytale when the same player scored the winner from the penalty spot.

NIGERIA 1994

The USA World Cup in 1994 was the first time that the Super Eagles played at the finals and what an impression they made. Drawn in a group with Argentina, Bulgaria and Greece, the African side defeated everybody but Argentina to qualify for the second round as group winners. There, they faced a hotly-tipped Italian side but the likes of Finidi George, Jay Jay Okocha and Daniel Amokachi, who later went on to play for Everton, showed what top players they were in an outstanding team performance. With the game in its 90th minute, Nigeria held a 1-0 lead thanks to a goal from Emmanuel

Senegal shocked World Cup holders France in the opening game of the 2002 World Cup

Amuneke but unfortunately for Nigeria, Roberto Baggio equalised just before the final whistle to send the game into extra-time. The same player then destroyed African dreams with a winner from the penalty spot.

SENEGAL 2002

Just like Cameroon 12 years before them, Senegal came into the first game of the 2002 World Cup in Japan/South Korea as rank outsiders against France, the defending champions, but just like their African neighbours before them, they caused a shock by winning 1-0 thanks to a goal from Papa Bouba Diop. Draws against Denmark and Uruguay then ensured Senegal's presence in the second round, where they beat Sweden 2-1 after extra time thanks to two goals from Henri Camara. In the quarter-finals they were paired with Turkey and after 90 minutes, the game remained deadlocked at 0-0. However a goal early in extra-time from Ilhan Mansiz gave Turkey a 1-0 victory, denying Senegal a spot in the semi-finals.

FAN-TASTIC

Sometimes the action in the stands at a World Cup is as colourful, stylish and exciting as that on the pitch – and sometimes it's just downright mad! Here's our guide to the supporters you're likely to see at South Africa 2010

SOUTH AFRICA

The piercing noise of the Vuvuzela – the plastic, metre-long horn of South African supporters which sounds like a swarm of overexcited bees – will provide the soundtrack to this summer's tournament. Many viewers will find it annoying when fans of the Bafana Bafana blow the instrument for 90 minutes at a time but no matter what you think of the noise they make, there's no doubting the passion of the home support.

South African football fans like to dress in outrageous colours and are unlikely to sit still during any of their team's games. Keep an eye out for the noise and passion when the hosts take on France in Bloemfontein in their final group game. The support in the Free State Stadium is noted for being the loudest and craziest in South Africa – France won't know what hit them. If Bafana Bafana need a result to stay in the tournament, it's the best venue for them to get it.

MEXICO

It might be a cliché but there are going to be a fair few moustached men with sombreros on their heads in the stands whenever Mexico take to the pitch. Although the Mexican support is predicted to be light in numbers this summer, they will make their presence felt and perhaps they will encourage fans in South Africa to start up a wave, a trend they made popular across the whole world during the 1986 World Cup.

URUGUAY

Like their Argentinean neighbours, Uruguay's football fans are a passionate bunch. The domestic league in the country may be littered with violent incidents but that has never transferred to the international scene. With a population of just over four million people, they won't be filling too many stadiums in South Africa but those who are there will certainly make their presence felt.

FRANCE

The phrases 'French Football' and 'passionate fans' don't normally go together – supporters of Les Bleus are just as likely to get on their team's back with a series of wolf-whistles than cheer them on when the team play at the Stade de France. But if things are going well on the pitch – and France don't have to resort to using their hands to win matches – their fans can be as loud as any other, as the 1998 World Cup helped prove. However it is not yet known if they will be able to sneak their famous cockerel mascot through South African customs.

ARGENTINA

Anyone who has been fortunate to attend a football match in Argentina will know what to expect from the country's fans at the World Cup. They jump up and down and chant like overexcited children during games, and like to get themselves into position in the stands hours before kick-off. Few groups of fans will match

the ferocity of their support during the tournament.

NIGERIA

Fans of the Super Eagles have stood out at the previous World Cup's their country have played courtesy of their bright green colours and passionate support. With Ireland's absence from the tournament, the Nigerian support in South Africa, which is expected to be massive, will take on the mantle of the biggest Guinness drinkers in South Africa on account of the 350 million pints they sink as a nation each year.

SOUTH KOREA

They may be relatively new to the international arena but South Korea's fans sure now how to put on a coordinated show. Wherever they play in South Africa each and every one of their fans will be dressed in red, and it's also interesting to note that they'll have a higher percentage of women supporters than any other country.

FAN-TASTIC

GREECE

It is just six years since Greek supporters went crazy in Portugal after their country won the European Championships and thousands of optimistic supporters will travel to South Africa in the hope that kind of achievement can be replicated.

ENGLAND

Fabio Capello's side will be one of the best supported countries in the tournament outside of the African nations. An estimated 40,000 are expected to pop over to South Africa at some stage during the World Cup and the FA will be expecting those who travel to be on their best behaviour, as they have been in recent tournaments. England's supporter band will also be there to play "the Great Escape" about 20 times over the course of every game.

USA

Football supporters in the US are a rare breed but those who are devoted to the game on the other side of the Atlantic are a dedicated bunch. They are expected to travel to South Africa in big numbers and prepare yourself for loud cries of "USA, USA" over and over again wherever they play throughout the tournament, or a chorus of "Our Legs Shall Never Tire, Our Hearts Will See Us Through, Goals! Goals! Goals! For the Red, White, and Blue", their official chant for the last World Cup.

African supporters and don't stop singing, dancing and beating drums. Despite their strong squad for this tournament, Ghanaian supporters are pessimists by nature and don't expect their side to go too far in the World Cup. But they will enjoy it as an experience and celebrate everything their team do.

AUSTRALIA

Football may not be the number one sport in Australia but the Socceroos won't be short of support during the World Cup. There is a large Australian community situated in South Africa which should lead to their matches being noisy and boisterous affairs. Expect Waltzing Matilda to be given an airing at some point.

ALGERIA

The most noteworthy thing about Algeria's World Cup play-off victory over Egypt last year was the violence that surrounded the game. But fear not – Algeria and Egypt have a particularly troublesome past and such events are unlikely to occur in South Africa. As you can probably tell, Algeria fans are particularly passionate about their team and will be most vocal in their support during the game against England on 18 June.

SLOVENIA

The smallest country at the World Cup will have one of the loudest sets of supporters at the tournament. A friendly game against Italy in 2002 had to be stopped because of the amount of fireworks and flares that were thrown onto the pitch, but that only goes to show the fans' passion for their team. They like to sing, too, and you can expect to spot and hear one or two accordions in the stands when Slovenia play.

GERMANY

Tens of thousands of German fans are expected in South Africa for the tournament. They will, as ever, be a lively bunch, their mood helped by swigging back a few beers before kick-off.

GHANA

Ghanaian fans are full of colour and life like many

SERBIA

Serbia has one of the biggest hooligan problems in European football but when travelling away from home, the Partizan and Red Star Belgrade rivalry is rarely a problem. Serbian fans may look tough but those who do travel to South Africa this summer will be on their best behaviour.

THE NETHERLANDS

Dutch supporters have been warned not to wear bright orange when they are out and about during the World Cup as it will make them stand out as a target for criminals. However, there'll be no stopping them on match day, when entire stadiums will appear to have been taken over by an army of tango men.

DENMARK

Danish supporters have a reputation as being among the best the world. In the 1980s, they travelled to support their country at major tournaments and named themselves "roligans" (rolig is the Danish word for calm) in opposition to the many hooligan groups that were following major countries at the time. They will travel to South Africa in big numbers and in great humour.

JAPAN

Japanese football fans have become more fervent since the foundation of the J League in the 1990s and represent a highly-organised group, with specially designed giant flags and banners a common site at matches. They also like to see Japanese cultural values replicated on the football pitch, so passing is valued over selfish play.

CAMEROON

Cameroon's colourful supporters will be back at the World Cup for the first time since 2002 and they'll be determined to enjoy the experience. Like all football fans from the continent, they will create an incredible atmosphere during their country's matches this summer. They can also count on support from their hosts in South Africa, who have always got behind Cameroon in previous World Cups.

ITALY

The passion for the game among Italian supporters is as strong as it is anywhere else in the world. During the qualifying campaign for the tournament, Italian manager Marcello Lippi was booed everywhere he went because he refused to select striker Antonio Cassano in his side. That shows that Italian fans don't tolerate poor decisions and while they'll get behind their side in South Africa, don't expect them to keep their mouths shut if their team fails to perform.

PARAGUAY

Paraguay's lack of international success has usually meant their supporters are a downbeat lot but they will head into this World Cup in optimistic mood having beaten both Argentina and Brazil in the qualifying campaign. There aren't too many supporters expected to travel to the tournament but those who are there will be every bit as fanatical as the supporters of other countries from South America.

BRAZIL

It just wouldn't be a World Cup without Brazil's samba-dancing supporters shaking their hips in the stands to create a carnival atmosphere. Usually they have an awful lot to be happy about but their energy and noise can bring even the dullest game to life. And watch out for TV cameramen focusing their lens on the throngs of beautiful Brazilian women who regularly travel to watch their team at major finals.

NEW ZEALAND

The first ever match of the All Whites to sell-out was their World Cup play-off match against Bahrain last year which suggests that the New Zealand public remain obsessed by rugby and cricket rather than football. However, the interest in the team amongst the country has increased dramatically since they qualified and a healthy number of supporters are expected to travel to South Africa to get behind their side.

SLOVAKIA

This will be Slovakia's first World Cup as an independent nation. Like many supporters from the same region – Slovenia and Serbia – they are a tough looking bunch but on the international scene, they have always been well behaved. Expect to see hundreds of tattoo-clad men with their tops off during their games.

IVORY COAST

Civil war has dominated the landscape of the Ivory Coast over the past few decades but even when the troubles were at their worst, both sides would always come together to lend their support to their national football team. Like all of the African countries, their support will be loud and colourful, helped by the wearing of traditional costumes and body paint.

PORTUGAL

Portuguese football fans are incredibly passionate and bring a samba atmosphere with them to games that is not dissimilar to that of Brazilian fans. They bring plenty of colour to football stadiums and for them football is a national obsession, a way of life. Don't miss the group game between the two countries on 25 June, which is sure to play host to one of the best atmospheres of the entire World Cup.

NORTH KOREA

Due to the strict exit laws that exist in their country, there are likely to only be a handful of North Korean supporters in South Africa for the World Cup. In fact matches at the tournament will not be shown live on TV just in case a defeat dampens the mood of the nation. Perhaps it's no harm that there will be few supporters at the tournament – the chant of "Chosun Igyura" meaning "Come on Korea" is about the only song that the fans sing at matches.

SPAIN

A passionate crew, Spanish fans are generally non-violent and enjoy the game as a spectacle rather than seeing it as a chance to drink and hang out with friends. They'll travel to South Africa with genuine hopes of winning the tournament

SWITZERLAND

Football in Switzerland has always been a sport for the family to enjoy together and the country's supporters have a reputation for being friendly and easy to approach. As a country famed for its neutrality, they are not the loudest bunch of supporters but expect them to get outraged if their game doesn't kick off on time.

CHILE

For a country recently hit by a football depression, the national game is now on the up in Chile and fans are more optimistic about the future of Chilean football and excited by their team once again. Like their South American counterparts, Chile's matches in the will be played to a soundtrack of music and drums.

HONDURAS

Honduras has been in turmoil since the president was ousted by the army last year, with the country's citizens being forced to obey nightly curfews, but the success of the football team has kept the nation's spirits up. When Honduras qualified for the World Cup, the new president declared a two-day holiday and those supporters lucky enough to get to South Africa this summer will be determined for the party to continue.

THE BIG WORLD CUP GUIDE

CONTENTS

THE STADIUMS 42

HIGH AND MIGHTY

The World Cup will be played in some of the most spectacular football (and rugby!) stadiums in the world – several of them at energy-sapping altitude!

Seven of this summer's World Cup venues are located at altitude, which is going to have a serious effect on the stamina of the players taking part in the tournament. The highest of all the altitude venues are the two in Johannesburg, the Soccer City Stadium and Ellis Park, which are both situated 5,570 feet above sea level. England, meanwhile, will start their campaign playing at

The magnificent Green Point Stadium in Cape Town

5,000 feet above the sea at the Royal Bafokeng Stadium in Rustenburg and are expected to play most of their matches in the knock-out stages at altitude if they manage to progress that far.

That is exactly why Fabio Capello is putting so much effort into ensuring that his players get their preparations for the tournament exactly right. The higher up you go from sea level, the less oxygen there is in the air which can have considerable knock-on effects. Firstly, players will have to breathe faster in order to maximise the amount of oxygen that goes from their lungs into

the bloodstream and secondly, their hearts will have to pump more to increase the supply of oxygen to the muscles. The overall effect is that players will become more tired more quickly which is why all teams will undergo altitude training in advance of the World Cup.

"It feels as though somebody has flicked a switch in your body," explained Shaun Edwards, one of the coaches of the British and Irish Lions rugby squad who toured South Africa in the summer of 2009. "Playing and training is still not easy but once you are acclimatised, it is much less difficult. For anybody who has not suffered the effects of playing up in the clouds, it's probably best described by trying to imagine a red-hot cup of tea being thrown down your airpipes every time you breath. It feels as if you have a chest infection and you tire during games very quickly."

The British and Irish Lions medical team advise that it took 10 to 14 days for their players to adjust to altitude, although some players struggled to cope during games no matter how hard they trained beforehand. That task will prove easier for players from a country like Chile, who play all their home matches at high altitude while English players, where the highest ground in the country is West Brom's The Hawthorns at 550 feet above sea level, may find it difficult to maintain the same energy levels.

There are also some crucial differences to how the ball will behave when it's struck at altitude. Because of the lack of oxygen in the air, the laws of physics dictate that the ball will travel further when kicked because there are less particles in the air to slow it down. Scientists expect the average ball to travel five per cent further and faster at altitude during the World Cup. But at altitude any free-kick or shot struck by the likes of Ronaldo and David Beckham will swerve less than it would at sea level.

The Soccer City Stadium, located not far from the township of Soweto in south-west Johannesburg, is the World Cup's most iconic venue. It is an upgrade of the old 80-000 capacity Soccer City stadium, a venue that hosted Nelson Mandela's first mass rally after his release from prison in 1990 and home to the Kaizer Chiefs, as well as the South African national football team. The ground's impressive new metallic exterior design has been inspired by an African cooking pot called the calabash, and the stadium will be lit at night to make it stand out even more on the Johannesburg skyline.

SOCCER CITY STADIUM, JOHANNESBURG

Elevation: 5,570 feet above sea level
Capacity: 94,700
Matches: Group games, second round, quarter-final, final

Ellis Park is located right in the centre of Johannesburg and is one of two rugby union stadiums that will be used during the World Cup. It was first built in 1928 and was completely demolished and reconstructed in 1982. The stadium holds a special place in the hearts of post-apartheid South Africa as it was here that Nelson Mandela presented Springbok captain Francois Pienaar with the Rugby World Cup trophy in 1995. Five thousand new seats have been added to bring capacity up to 62,000 for the World Cup. It is also home to the Orlando Pirates.

ELLIS PARK (COCA COLA PARK), JOHANNESBURG

Elevation: 5,570 feet above sea level
Capacity: 62,000
Matches: Group games, second round, quarter-final

MBOMBELA STADIUM,
NELSPRUIT

Elevation: 2,220 feet above sea level
Capacity: 46,000
Matches: Group games

The Mbombela Stadium is one of the World Cup's newly-built venues. It is located five miles from the city of Nelspruit, 60 miles from Johannesburg and is in close proximity to many game parks and reserves, which explains why the stadium's seats have a zebra pattern. Nelspruit itself is a picturesque city with a whole host of museums, monuments and other historical buildings.

PETER MOKABA
STADIUM, POLOKWANE

Elevation: 4,206 feet above sea level
Capacity: 46,000
Matches: Group games

Another newly-built venue, the Peter Mokoba stadium is named after a local activist who played a huge part in South Africa's struggle against the apartheid regime. The stadium's design is inspired by the local Baobab tree, with the steel structured roof being supported by giant 'trunks' at each corner of the stadium. The city itself is known as South Africa's safest provincial capital and the translation of its name into English, "place of safety", gives that away. Polokwane is surrounded by farms, orchards and ranches which should make it a popular destination for fans.

Another rugby stadium, Loftus Versfeld is one of the oldest sporting venues in South Africa. It has been used for sporting events since 1903 and has undergone regular reconstruction work through the years. It is home to the Blue Bulls rugby team, as well as ABSA Premiership teams Mamelodi Sundowns and SuperSport United. It also has a special place in the heart of all Bafana Bafana supporters – it was here that the team recorded their first victory against a European side in an encounter with Sweden in 1999.

LOFTUS VERSFELD STADIUM, PRETORIA

Elevation: 4,500 feet above sea level
Capacity: 50,000
Matches: Group games, second round

The venue for England's opening game has only needed a small upgrade to bring it up to World Cup standards. It is situated 25 minutes from the Sun City resort, nine miles from Rustenburg city centre and just a few minutes drive from England's training base. The stadium is named after the Bafokeng people, who live in the area and are entitled to 20 per cent of the proceeds from all platinum mining in the area.

ROYAL BAFOKENG STADIUM, RUSTENBURG

Elevation: 5,000 feet above sea level
Capacity: 42,000
Matches: Group games, second round

THE STADIUMS

FREE STATE STADIUM, BLOEMFONTEIN

Elevation: 4,500 feet above sea level
Capacity: 48,000
Matches: Group games, second round

The Free State Stadium has had 10,000 extra seats added in preparation for the World Cup and is expected to be one of the noisiest of all venues because of the renowned passion of the local support. It is currently home to rugby's Free State Cheetahs and football's Bloemfontein Celtic, two teams that have become extremely popular in their respective sports in recent years. Situated in the centre of the country, Bloemfontein is a crossroads for the entire nation and is the judicial capital of South Africa.

MOSES MABHIDA STADIUM, DURBAN

Elevation: Sea level
Capacity: 70,000
Matches: Group games, second round, semi-final

This spectacular newly-built stadium in South Africa's third largest city has a grand arch much like Wembley's but it hosts one additional feature. A cable car can ascend to a viewing platform on top of the arch 106 metres above the ground, offering spectacular views of the nearby shoreline. In addition to a stadium that boasts the best pitch views of any other in the tournament, the venue will also house restaurants, bars and a pedestrian walkway linking the stadium to the beach.

The brand new Nelson Madela Bay Stadium is the first football dedicated stadium in the entire Port Elizabeth region. It was also the first new venue – with its iconic roof – to be completed in South Africa, a full year before the start of the World Cup too. Port Elizabeth itself is sandwiched between the shores of the North End lake and the Indian Ocean and is known as the watersports capital of the country.

NELSON MANDELA BAY STADIUM, PORT ELIZABETH

Elevation: Sea level
Capacity: 48,000
Matches: Group stages, second round, quarter-final, 3rd/4th placed play-off

Situated just a few hundred metres from both the sea and mountains of Cape Town, this newly-built venue is one of the most picturesque in the tournament. The stadium has an exterior covered in noise-reducing cladding to ensure sound reverberates around the venue and has been constructed on what used to be a golf course. After the World Cup, the stadium will be used by local football sides Ajax Cape Town and Santos, as well as hosting concerts and other major events.

GREEN POINT STADIUM, CAPE TOWN

Elevation: Sea level
Capacity: 70,000
Matches: Group games, second round, quarter-finals, semi-finals

SOUTH AFRICA

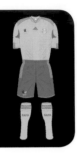

South Africa will enjoy the advantage of being the host nation at the World Cup, and their noisy, excitable supporters are sure to create a fantastic atmosphere during all their team's matches. However, Bafana Bafana ('The Boys, The Boys'), as they are known, are the lowest-ranked country at the tournament, so the odds are very much stacked against them.

South Africa's preparations for the tournament were thrown into disarray when their recently appointed coach, the Brazilian Carlos Alberto Parreira, quit the job in 2008 for family reasons. Another Brazilian, Joel Santana, took over and guided Bafana Bafana to a creditable fourth place at the 2009 Confederations Cup and, for a while, South Africa appeared to be back on course.

However, Santana then seemed to lose the plot completely, trying out over 30 players in four friendlies, all of which were lost to send the team's confidence slumping to a new low. The South African FA eventually

> **"Our group is the only one containing two former champions – France and Uruguay. This group is a challenge."**
> South Africa coach Carlos Alberto Parreira

lost patience, and in October 2009 replaced him with Parreira, their original choice as coach back in 2007.

This somewhat bewildering chain of events has not left the hosts much time to get their act together. Parreira, though, was helped by the shutting down of the domestic league in January 2010 which allowed him to take his locally-based players away to a training camp. However, many of the team's most important players play for clubs overseas: among them Everton's hard-working midfielder Steven Pienaar, Portsmouth hardman Aaron Mokoena, Blackburn striker Benni McCarthy and Arminia Bielefeld goalkeeper Rowen Fernandez.

The hosts usually do well at the World Cup, but it's difficult to see South Africa maintaining this tradition as their team lacks international-class performers in virtually all departments. Sadly for their fans, the party could be over pretty quickly.

THE GAFFER: CARLOS ALBERTO PARREIRA

Of all the coaches at the World Cup, South Africa's Carlos Alberto Parreira will easily be the most experienced, having led four different countries at five previous tournaments. Most famously, the 67-year-old Brazilian guided his home country to success in the 1994 World Cup in the USA, and was also in charge of the South Americans when they fared rather less well four years ago in Germany. His other three World Cup campaigns, meanwhile, were with Kuwait (1982), United Arab Emirates (1990) and Saudi Arabia (1998).
Parreira is in his second spell as South Africa coach, having left the post in 2008 to care for his sick wife. He was re-appointed to the role in October 2009 after the previous incumbent, fellow Brazilian Joel Santana, was dismissed following a dismal run of results. Parreira had an instant impact, tightening up a leaky defence to enable South Africa to claim morale-boosting 0-0 draws with Japan and Jamaica.
   However, despite the marked improvement in the team's displays, Parreira's return has been strongly criticised by some inside South Africa who were disappointed a local coach did not get the opportunity to lead Bafana Bafana at the finals.

KEY PLAYER:
AARON MOKOENA

A versatile player who can perform equally well in central defence or as a holding midfielder, South Africa captain Aaron Mokoena is a central figure for Bafana Bafana. His country's youngest ever international when he made his debut aged 18 in 1999, Mokoena is now one of the elder statesmen in the squad and his experience will be a major asset to the host nation. Nicknamed 'The Axe' for his rugged tackling, Mokoena started out with local clubs Jomo Cosmos and Ajax Cape Town, before signing for Bayer Leverkusen. However, he failed to break into the Germans' first team and soon moved on to Ajax where, again, his opportunities were limited. His career picked up, though, when he tried his luck in Belgium, first with Germinal Beerschot and then with Genk. In 2005 Blackburn splashed out £600,000 to bring him to Ewood Park, where he gained a reputation as an energetic, whole-hearted and ultra-competitive performer before joining Portsmouth on a free transfer in the summer of 2009.

ONE TO WATCH:
TEKO MODISE

An attacking midfielder whose slight frame, expert close control and mazy dribbling skills have earned him the nickname 'Deco', after the veteran Portuguese playmaker, Teko Modise is a huge favourite with South African fans. Born in Soweto 27 years ago, Modise plays for Orlando Pirates in South Africa's Premier Soccer League. His consistently excellent performances for his club won him the PSL Footballer of the Year award in both 2008 and 2009, and attracted interest from a number of leading European clubs, including Aston Villa, Manchester City and both Milans.

Modise made his debut for Bafana Bafana against Malawai in the 2007 COSAFA Cup, an annual tournament for southern African nations. He has since gone on to win over 40 caps, making him one of the more experienced players in a young South African team. The most likely source of goals for his country from midfield, Modise is an excellent finisher inside the box who can also strike from long range. With nine goals already for his country, he will be hoping to get into double figures at the World Cup.

TACTICS BOARD:
GOALS REQUIRED

Brazilian coach Carlos Alberto Parreira will send out the home side in a 4-4-2 formation in a bid to get the goals that South Africa will need if they are to make it through to the second round.

One of Bafana Bafana's problems, though, is that a strike partnership of Blackburn veteran Benni McCarthy and Mamelodi Sundowns' Katlego Mphela will not cause top-class defences too many worries on their own, so the South African midfielders will need to give them support. Orlando Pirates' Teko Modise will probably make most forward forays from this area, as central midfielders Steven Pienaar and Fulham's Kagisho Dikgacoi will be concerned about leaving a vulnerable-looking defence exposed to the counter-attack.

However, South Africa's all-round lack of quality means they will probably have to play more defensively than Parreira would like especially if, as seems likely, the opposition dominate possession for large periods.

SOUTH AFRICA AT THE WORLD CUP

The World Cup hasn't been a happy hunting ground for South Africa

• 2010 hosts South Africa do not have much of a World Cup history to look back on. The country did not enter the tournament between 1930-62 and was then banned from entering by FIFA until after the 1990 tournament because of the apartheid regime operating in South Africa at the time.

• **After missing out in 1994, South Africa first qualified for the World Cup in 1998. Their opening match was against hosts France, and defender Pierre Issa became the first South African to score at the tournament... sadly for him, the ball went in at the wrong end as Bafana Bafana slumped to a comprehensive 3-0 defeat.**

• South Africa did considerably better in their second match, drawing 1-1 with Denmark thanks to a second-half equaliser from striker Benni McCarthy. That result gave Bafana Bafana a chance of reaching the knock-out stage, but first they had to beat Saudi Arabia in their final match and hope that Denmark didn't take a point off France.

• **The French fulfilled their part of the equation, beating the Danes 2-1, but South Africa could only manage a 2-2 draw against the Saudis. Shaun Bartlett, who later** played in the Premiership for Charlton Athletic, scored both of South Africa's goals, the second an injury-time equaliser from the penalty spot.

• Four years later South Africa were back at the finals in Japan and South Korea. They began their campaign by fighting back from 2-0 down to draw 2-2 with Paraguay, Teboho Mokoena and Manchester United midfielder Quinton Fortune grabbing the all-important goals.

• **In their next match the South Africans recorded their first ever victory at the finals, Udinese's Siyabonga Nomventhe scoring the only goal of the game against** Slovenia after just four minutes. The three points put the Bafana Bafana second in their group, and meant they would need a point against already-qualified Spain in their final match to be certain of reaching the knock-out stages.

• South Africa fought hard against Spain, twice equalising through Benni McCarthy and Lucas Radebe before finally going down 3-2. In the other game, meanwhile, Paraguay beat Slovenia 3-1 to pip Bafana Bafana to second place on goals scored after the teams were tied on points and goal difference. It was a sad way for South Africa to bow out, but they had done the new multi-racial 'rainbow nation' proud.

PREVIOUS TOURNAMENTS

1930 Did not enter	1962 Did not enter	1986 Banned
1934 Did not enter	1966 Banned	1990 Banned
1938 Did not enter	1970 Banned	1994 Did not qualify
1950 Did not enter	1974 Banned	1998 Round 1
1954 Did not enter	1978 Banned	2002 Round 1
1958 Did not enter	1982 Banned	2006 Did not qualify

MEXICO

Mexico have a proud record at the World Cup, having appeared at 13 of the previous tournaments. And while the Central Americans have never progressed beyond the quarter-finals they are usually one of the most entertaining teams at the finals, playing a brand of attacking football that is full of latin flair.

For a while, though, it appeared unlikely that Mexico would be on the plane to South Africa. They had a poor start in their qualifying group under Sven Goran Eriksson, but results soon improved when the onetime England boss was unceremoniously sacked after just ten months in charge and replaced with Javier Aguirre, a former Mexican international who had coached the national team once before. Mexico eventually clinched their spot in the finals with an emphatic 4-1 victory over El Salvador – despite a swarm of bees in the penalty area holding up play for ten minutes.

> **"We play the hosts in the opening game of the World Cup and have to be in the best shape that's possible."**
>
> Mexico coach
> Javier Aguirre.

Aguirre generally favours an offensive 4-3-3 system, although he sometimes adapts the formation depending on the opponent. The front three may well feature two London-based strikers in Arsenal's Carlos Vela and West Ham's Guillermo Franco, a naturalized Mexican who was born in Argentina. Further back, the star of the midfield is Deportivo la Coruna's Andres Guardado, a talented player with excellent dribbling skills and a powerful left foot shot, while the lynchpin of the defence is Barcelona's Rafael Marquez. Goalkeeper Guillermo Ochoa of Mexican side Club America is another mainstay of the team, and has earned many plaudits for his shot-stopping skills.

Although maddeningly inconsistent, Mexico are a tricky side who will relish playing at high altitude. They will be desperate to get beyond the second round, having fallen at this hurdle at the last four World Cups.

MEXICO AT THE WORLD CUP

• After making little impression at previous tournaments, Mexico took advantage of their host nation status to reach the quarter-finals for the first time in 1970. In the group stage they scored one of the strangest World Cup goals ever when a Mexican player took a free-kick awarded to El Salvador, the ball eventually reaching Javier Valdivia who fired home. Bizarrely, the Egyptian referee allowed the goal to stand.

• **Hosting the tournament for a second time in 1986, Mexico again reached the quarter-finals before going out to West Germany on penalties after a dull 0-0 draw.**

• FIFA banned Mexico from the 1990 tournament after the central Americans fielded over-age players in the qualifiers for the 1988 Olympics. Since then the Mexicans have been remarkably consistent,

reaching the first knock-out round at the last four World Cups.

• **Mexican goalkeeper Antonio Carbajal was the first player to appear at five consecutive World Cups, featuring in the 1950, 1954, 1958, 1962 and 1966 tournaments. Altogether less impressively, he conceded a record 25 goals in the 11 games he played in.**

PREVIOUS TOURNAMENTS

1930 Round 1	1962 Round 1	1986 Quarter-finals
1934 Did not qualify	1966 Round 1	1990 Banned
1938 Withdrew	1970 Quarter-finals	1994 Round 2
1950 Round 1	1974 Did not qualify	1998 Round 2
1954 Round 1	1978 Round 1	2002 Round 2
1958 Round 1	1982 Did not qualify	2006 Round 2

KEY PLAYER:
RAFAEL MARQUEZ

Hugely experienced and an inspirational leader, Mexico captain Rafael Marquez is easily the most important player in his country's team. A versatile performer who can play in the centre of defence or in a defensive midfield role, Marquez is now approaching a century of caps having made his international debut as far back as 1997. The following year he missed out on selection for France '98 but he was an ever-present for Mexico at the following two World Cups.

Marquez began his club career with Mexican side Atlas before joining Monaco, with whom he won the French title in 2000. He moved on to Barcelona in 2003 and three years later became the first ever Mexican to win the Champions League when the Catalans defeated Arsenal in the final in Paris.

URUGUAY

The smallest country ever to win the World Cup, Uruguay have been world champions on two occasions, in 1930 and 1950. The South Americans' recent record, though, is much less impressive and their appearance in South Africa will only be their second at the finals in the last two decades. They will, no doubt, be desperate to make up for all those wasted years.

Uruguay were the last country to book their place at this summer's football party and they kept their supporters biting their nails until the very last minute. After a mediocre campaign The Celeste (Sky Blue) finished fifth in their qualifying group and were pitched into a two-leg play-off against Costa Rica. A 1-0 win in San Jose seemed to set them up perfectly for the home leg, but Uruguay could only manage a nervy 1-1 draw in Montevideo in the return. Still, it proved enough for the home side and their manager Oscar Tabarez, an experienced coach who was briefly in charge of AC Milan in the mid-1990s.

Uruguay's strengths are at opposite ends of the pitch, in defence and attack. In goal Juan Castillo, of Brazilian side Botofogo, is a steady performer, while in front of him captain Diego Lugano of Turkish giants Fenerbahce is a resolute stopper who leads his team by example. The South Americans' big stars, though, are their strikers, Atletico Madrid's Diego Forlan and 23-year-old Luis Suarez, a prolific scorer with Ajax. Uruguay's midfield is, perhaps, less impressive, although the left-footed Ignacio Gonzalez, who was briefly on Newcastle's books in 2008, is a firm fans' favourite.

An inconsistent and unpredictable team, Uruguay's chances in South Africa are hard to assess. However, if they play to their potential they should get past the group stage at the very least.

> **"I am happy to qualify, but not for the way we clinched it. It is unbelievable that we had to suffer that way."**
> Uruguay captain Diego Lugano

URUGUAY AT THE WORLD CUP

• In 1930 Uruguay became the first winners of the World Cup, beating arch-rivals Argentina 4-2 in the final on home soil in Montevideo. A dispute about which ball to use was solved when the teams agreed to use an Argentinean ball in the first half and a Uruguayan one in the second half.

• **Uruguay won the World Cup for a second time in 1950, defeating** hosts Brazil 2-1 in the 'final' (it was actually the last and decisive match in a four-team final group that also included Sweden and Spain). The match was watched by a huge crowd of 199,589 in the famous Maracana stadium in Rio de Janeiro, the largest ever to attend a football match anywhere in the world.

• Fours years later they recorded one of the biggest victories in World Cup history when they thrashed Scotland 7-0 in Switzerland. They went on to reach the semi-finals before losing 4-2 to Hungary.

• **Since then Uruguay's star has waned, although they did reach the semi-finals again in 1970 before losing 3-1 to eventual champions Brazil.**

PREVIOUS TOURNAMENTS

1930 Winners	1962 Round 1	1986 Round 2
1934 Withdrew	1966 Quarter-finals	1990 Round 2
1938 Did not enter	1970 Fourth place	1994 Did not qualify
1950 Winners	1974 Round 1	1998 Did not qualify
1954 Fourth place	1978 Did not qualify	2002 Round 1
1958 Did not qualify	1982 Did not qualify	2006 Did not qualify

KEY PLAYER:
DIEGO FORLAN

A nippy striker who packs an explosive shot, Diego Forlan is one of the most consistent goalscorers in world football. His total of seven goals in the qualifiers was vital to Uruguay's progress, especially a last-minute winner against Ecuador that booked their play-off place. It's strange to think, then, that Forlan was something of a joke figure during a largely dismal time with Manchester United, who he joined from Argentinean club Independiente for £6.9 million in 2002.

Forlan's fortunes changed, though, when he moved to Villarreal in 2004. The following season he topped the European scoring charts with Arsenal's Thierry Henry, much to the surprise of those who had seen him struggle at Old Trafford. In 2007 he moved on to Atletico Madrid, where he claimed another European Golden Boot after a goal-filled season in 2008/09.

FRANCE

Of all the nations heading to South Africa, France are by some distance the most fortunate. First, Les Bleus sneaked through the play-offs after beating Ireland thanks to a goal that should have been disallowed for a blatant handball by striker Thierry Henry. Then, they were handed a very favourable draw at the finals, landing in the same group as the weakest top seeds, hosts South Africa.

French coach Raymond Domenech, a keen astrologist, must be thanking his lucky stars. Under fire since a series of dire displays by his team at Euro 2008, he will want to draw a line under an equally unimpressive qualifying campaign, which culminated in the French reaching the finals in circumstances so controversial that even their own supporters were too embarrassed to celebrate. Needless to say, meanwhile, Ireland's bitterly disappointed fans will be praying that France make an early exit.

That could still happen because, with the eccentric

> **"The draw is quite balanced. We will play the host nation and this is never an easy task."**
> France coach Raymond Domenech

Domenech at the helm, France are not so much a team as a collection of gifted individuals. However, a side featuring the various attacking talents of Henry, Nicolas Anelka, Bayern Munich's Franck Ribery and Real Madrid's Karim Benzema can't be dismissed lightly. Indeed, with an additional cast of Madrid's Lassana Diarra in midfield and William Gallas, Patrice Evra and Bacary Sagna at the back, France should be classed as one of the World Cup favourites.

However, the French suffer from a severe lack of cohesion and organisation on the pitch which undermines their credentials as serious candidates. Just as damagingly, they are also divided between those players who remain loyal to Domenench, and those, including skipper Henry, who see him as a liability. Given this mixed bag of positives and negatives it's difficult to judge how France will fare, but their campaign will surely make interesting viewing.

THE GAFFER: RAYMOND DOMENECH

Despite taking his country to the World Cup final in 2006, and only losing the game on penalties, France coach Raymond Domenech has attracted more negative headlines than virtually any other manager in world football.

The French press have been calling for Domenech's head since a dismal showing by *Les Bleus* at Euro 2008, and they would almost certainly have had their wish but for the infamous Thierry Henry handball that took France to South Africa at the expense of Ireland. As well as overseeing a string of disappointing results and performances, Domenech is also accused of being tactically naïve and falling out too easily with certain players. Then, there is his bizarre admission that astrology plays a part in his team selections – Domenech, it is said, ended former Arsenal midfielder Robert Pires' international career simply because he is a Scorpio, a sign the French boss distrusts.

A former coach of the French Under-21 team who was a surprise choice to succeed Jacques Santini in 2004, Domenech will clearly be under huge pressure at the World Cup. But he has confounded his critics before and, if the planets align in his favour, may do so again.

KEY PLAYER:
FRANCK RIBERY

Described by the legendary Zinedine Zidane as 'the jewel of French football', Bayern Munich winger Franck Ribery is one the most coveted players in the world game. In the year leading up to the World Cup in South Africa Ribery was a target for Manchester United and Chelsea, the two Premiership giants apparently prepared to break the bank to bring the 2008 German Footballer of the Year to England. An energetic performer who has pace and skill in abundance, Ribery began his career with Boulogne, later moving to Metz. In 2005 he joined Galatasaray but, after going four months without pay, soon returned to France with Marseille. A magnificent season in 2006/07, when he scored 14 goals as Marseille finished second behind Lyon, was followed by a £20 million move to Bayern.

Ribery, whose scarred face is the result of serious car accident when he was just two years old, made his debut for France just before the 2006 World Cup. He played superbly at that tournament, and will be a major threat again this time around.

ONE TO WATCH: KARIM BENZEMA

Now a 'galactico' at Real Madrid, Karim Benzema came through the youth academy at Lyon to be hailed as a star of the future before he was out of his teens. Former French international striker Jean-Pierre Papin was among those to sing Benzema's praises, comparing the youngster to two Brazilian greats. "His power is reminiscent of Ronaldo," he enthused, "and the stepovers and speed at which he runs with the ball is like Ronaldinho."

For once, the hype was justified as Benzema established himself in the Lyon team, enjoying a brilliant season in 2007/08 when he scored 20 goals to help his club win a first ever league and cup double. A year later he was on his way to the Bernabeu, joining Real for a fee of around £32 million.

Benzema, whose parents are of Algerian descent, was approached to play for the north African country in December 2006 but turned the opportunity down, insisting that he would only represent France. Just three months later he was called up for a friendly against Austria, and marked his international debut by scoring the only goal of the game.

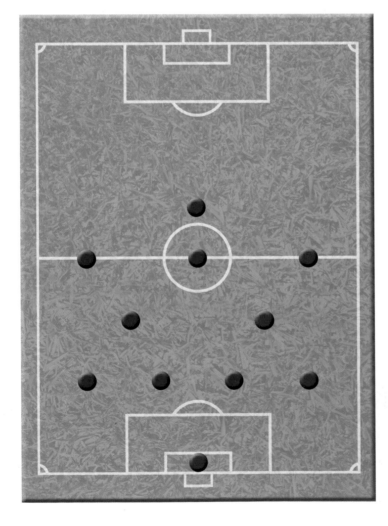

TACTICS BOARD:
DAZED & CONFUSED?

"We do not know how to play, where to be on the pitch, how to organise," lamented France star Thierry Henry recently. "We do not know what to do." Henry's complaints were aimed at coach Raymond Domenech, who usually favours a 4-2-3-1 formation with the Barcelona man one of the wide players behind a single striker, Toulouse forward Andre-Pierre Gignan filling this role in the play-off against Ireland. The return of Franck Ribery from injury, though, could see Nicholas Anelka moving from the flank to the centre, with Bordeaux playmaker Yoann Gourcuff dropping in behind him. Karim Benzema is another option up top, but the Real Madrid star is more likely to start on the bench. In midfield, Lassana Diarra and Lyon's Jeremy Toulalan are a pair of dependable workhorses while, at the back in front of Lyon goalkeeper Hugo Lloris, Domenech has attracted yet more criticism by sometimes selecting a left-back, Barcelona's Eric Abidal, alongside William Gallas.

FRANCE AT THE WORLD CUP

• France played in the first ever World Cup match, beating Mexico 4-1 in Montevideo, Uruguay on 13 July 1930. In front of a crowd of just 3,000 in the Pocitos stadium, France's Lucien Laurent scored the tournament's first ever goal after 19 minutes.

• In the same tournament France were trailing 1-0 to Argentina when the Brazilian referee blew the final whistle after 84 minutes. Following protests from the French players, the ref realised his mistake and the final six minutes were played out with no change in the scoreline.

• In 1938 France hosted the tournament for the first time, with ten different cities acting as venues. For the first time in World Cup history the hosts failed to win, France losing to reigning champions and eventual winners Italy in the quarter-finals.

• In Sweden in 1958 France finished in third place after losing 5-2 in the semi-finals to eventual champions Brazil. Their striker Just Fontaine set a record for the tournament by scoring 13 goals, including a hat-trick against Paraguay and four goals against West Germany in the play-off for third place.

Zinedane Zidane examines the World Cup trophy in 1998

• France reached the semi-finals again in 1982, but lost the first ever penalty shoot-out at the World Cup to West Germany after a thrilling 3-3 draw. The match, though, is also remembered for an appalling forearm smash by German goalkeeper Harald Schumacher on Patrick Battiston which knocked out three of the Frenchman's teeth and left him unconscious. Incredibly, the referee didn't even blow for a foul.

• After another semi-final defeat in 1986, France eventually reached the final for the first time as hosts in 1998. Their opponents, reigning champions Brazil, were easily swept aside, star player Zinedine Zidane scoring with two headers and Emmanuel Petit adding a third late on as France won 3-0. After the match more than a million people took to the streets of Paris to celebrate the country's success.

• Four years later, though, France put up a limp defence of their trophy, crashing out in the first round after surprise defeats by Senegal and Denmark.

• Les Bleus were back on form in 2006, reaching the final in Germany where they were unfortunate to lose out to Italy in a penalty shoot-out. Sadly, the magnificent career of the great Zinedine Zidane ended on a sour note when he was sent off for headbutting Italian defender Marco Materazzi.

PREVIOUS TOURNAMENTS

1930 Round 1	1962 Did not qualify	1986 Third place
1934 Round 1	1966 Round 1	1990 Did not qualify
1938 Round 2	1970 Did not qualify	1994 Did not qualify
1950 Did not qualify	1974 Did not qualify	1998 Winners
1954 Round 1	1978 Round 1	2002 Round 1
1958 Third place	1982 Fourth place	2006 Runners-up

ARGENTINA

With the dazzling Lionel Messi, the reigning World Footballer of the Year, and a host of other big-name players in their ranks, Argentina will be a team to watch this summer. The South Americans are two-time winners of the World Cup and would love to make it a treble in South Africa, but their form going into the finals is distinctly patchy.

Indeed, as the qualification process drew to a close there was a strong possibility that the Argentinean players would be watching the tournament at home on TV. Three consecutive defeats against Ecuador, Brazil and Paraguay left Diego Maradona's squad in a grim situation but they eventually squeezed into the last automatic qualifying slot in the South American section after winning their final two games.

> **"Greece is a former European champion – we won't expect an easy opening round."**
>
> Argentina striker Gonzalo Higuain

Argentina may not be as strong as they have been in the past, but a team which boasts the attacking talents of Messi, Atletico Madrid's Sergio Aguero, Real Madrid hitman Gonzalo Higuain and former Manchester United playmaker Juan Sebastian Veron has to be taken seriously.

However, the *Albicelestes* ('White and Sky Blues') could be hamstrung by a defence that has looked extremely vulnerable, notably when conceding six goals to Bolivia in one of their six defeats in qualifying. Former Manchester United full-back Gabriel Heinze is one of the regulars in the back four, but he now looks past his best as does 36-year-old veteran Javier Zanetti.

The tactics and selections of Maradona have also generated a great deal of criticism, and the coach's lack of experience allied to his unpredictable temperament means he could prove to be something of a liability to his team.

Given these various handicaps, the *Albicelestes* might well struggle in South Africa. If one of the big boys does go out at the group stage it could easily be Argentina.

THE GAFFER: DIEGO MARADONA

An icon in Argentina who is considered by many fans throughout the world the greatest footballer ever, Diego Maradona has endured a torrid time since being made his country's coach in November 2008.

Argentina were struggling in their World Cup qualifying group at the time, but their form lurched alarmingly during Maradona's initial months in charge, a 6-1 defeat in Bolivia equalling the Albicelestes' worst ever defeat. With Argentina's qualification hopes hanging in the balance, his critics called for him to stand down, pointing to a lack of team strategy and inexplicable selections in their case against the 1986 World Cup-winning captain. Maradona, though, had the last laugh as Argentina claimed the fourth qualifying spot in their group after consecutive last-gasp wins against Peru and Uruguay. He let off steam in typical Maradona fashion, with a foul-mouthed rant in a post-match press conference which earned him a two-month ban from football.

As a player, Maradona was supreme; however, he has very little experience as a coach and is notoriously volatile. How he copes with the pressure-cooker atmosphere in South Africa will be one of the summer's most fascinating sub-plots.

KEY PLAYER:
LIONEL MESSI

The reigning World Player of the Year, Lionel Messi should be one of the stars of this summer's World Cup. However, he has sometimes struggled to reproduce the form he has shown for his club, Barcelona, at international level, most notably during a disappointing qualifying campaign.

A brilliant dribbler whose jinking runs are a delight to watch, Messi has not been helped by Argentina's long ball tactics that have left him looking an isolated and frustrated figure at times. He will hope that coach Diego Maradona, ironically a player very much in Messi's mould in his heyday, will devise a strategy that allows him to show off his dazzling skills on the world stage. Certainly, it would be a terrible shame if the 22-year-old's outrageous talent was not given the right platform to flourish.

Messi has had no such problems at club level, where he has enjoyed great success with Barcelona, particularly in the 2008/09 season when he helped the Catalan giants win the domestic double and the Champions League.

ONE TO WATCH: GONZALO HIGUAIN

The son of a former Argentine footballer, Gonzalo Higuain was born in northern France and originally seemed set to play for Les Bleus. He was given the number 20 shirt ahead of a game against Greece in November 2006, but at the last minute had a change of heart, deciding to commit his international future to Argentina. After representing the Argentina Olympic team in February 2008 he made his full debut in a World Cup qualifier against Peru in Buenos Aires the following year, scoring a goal in a vital 2-1 victory for his country.

A pacy striker with quick feet who specializes in hard, low drives, Higuain began his club career in 2004 with River Plate, one of his father's former clubs. In January 2007 he moved to Real Madrid for around £11 million, and has since averaged a goal every other game for the Spanish giants. He helped Madrid win the league title in both 2007 and 2008, before cementing his reputation as one of the world's most promising forwards by notching a career best 22 league goals in 2008/09.

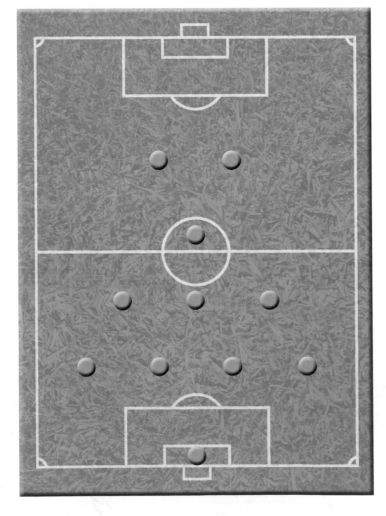

TACTICS BOARD:
MESSI CONNECTIONS

Coach Diego Maradona will send out his Argentina team either in a traditional 4-4-2 or a 4-3-1-2 formation. In the latter system Juan Sebastian Veron will play as an advanced midfielder, where he will attempt to make use of his perceptive passing to set up chances for Lionel Messi and either Sergio Aguero or Gonzalo Higuain. Messi, Argentina's star player, might find this set-up to his liking as he has a good understanding with Veron. In the centre of midfield, the tigerish Javier Mascherano has a ball-winning role in front of the defence while Newcastle's Jonas Guiterrez and Benfica's Angel di Maria are a hard-running pair down the flanks.

If Argentina are to prosper the defence will need to distribute the ball more accurately than they did in the qualifiers, when they often resorted to long, high balls which sailed over a perplexed Messi's head. The little genius needs better service than that if he is to shine.

ARGENTINA AT THE WORLD CUP

• Argentina appeared in the first ever World Cup final, but lost 4-2 to neighbours Uruguay in Montevideo. The result went down badly in Buenos Aires, where the Uruguayan Consulate was stoned by an angry mob until the police turned up and opened fire on the crowd.

• **After a 24-year absence Argentina returned to the finals in 1958 with a side full of talented players. However, they were unsophisticated tactically and finished bottom of their group after losing their final match 6-1 to Czechoslovakia. The humiliation was too much to bear for the Argentinean public who pelted the team with coins and vegetables on their return from Sweden.**

• Eight years later, Argentina were involved in one of the most notorious matches in World Cup history when they faced hosts England in the quarter-finals at Wembley. Their captain Antonio Rattin was sent off in the first half, but refused to leave the pitch for some minutes. After a bruising match, which the South Americans lost 1-0, England manager Alf Ramsey branded the Argentineans 'animals'.

• **In 1978 Argentina hosted the tournament for the first time**

Maradona runs rings around England in 1986

and, spurred on by a fanatical, confetti-throwing home crowd, stormed to victory in the final against Holland. Striker Mario Kempes was the hero of the hour, with two goals in his team's 3-1 victory.

• After a disappointing showing in 1982, Argentina won the World Cup for a second time in 1986 in Mexico. Their inspiration was the brilliant Diego Maradona, who dragged an otherwise fairly ordinary team through to the final, scoring magnificent individual goals against England and Belgium. Less impressively, Maradona also punched in a goal against the English, although he later cheekily claimed that it had been scored with 'The Hand of God'. In an

exciting final Argentina beat West Germany 3-2, Jorge Burruchaga scoring the winner five minutes from the end from Maradona's superb pass.

• **Four years later Argentina reached the final for a fourth time, but lost 1-0 to West Germany in a dire match. In the 65th minute Argentina's Pedro Monzon became the first player to be sent off in a World Cup final, and he was later followed by team-mate Gustavo Dezotti who received a red card in the final minutes.**

• At the 2006 World Cup Argentina were hotly tipped, especially after trouncing Serbia 6-0, but they surprisingly went out to Germany in the quarter-finals.

PREVIOUS TOURNAMENTS

1930 Runners-up	1962 Round 1	1986 Winners
1934 Round 1	1966 Quarter-finals	1990 Runners-up
1938 Withdrew	1970 Did not qualify	1994 Round 2
1950 Did not enter	1974 Round 2	1998 Quarter-finals
1954 Did not enter	1978 Winners	2002 Round 1
1958 Round 1	1982 Round 2	2006 Quarter-finals

NIGERIA

A strong side containing a host of Premiership players, Nigeria will be a danger to any team in the tournament. The Super Eagles will be particularly keen to do well in the summer having failed to qualify for the finals last time around, while the draw has revived memories of their World Cup debut in 1994 when they were also paired with Argentina and Greece.

Nigeria, though, only made it to South Africa by the skin of their teeth. Needing a win away to Kenya to have any chance of pipping Tunisia, the Super Eagles recovered from a goal down to lead 2-1 before being pegged back to 2-2. However, a second goal from substitute Obafemi Martins gave them the points that, combined with Tunisia's surprising defeat in Mozambique, booked their place at the finals.

On the face of it, Nigeria should have qualified with far greater ease. Their squad is packed full of talented players, including Everton defender Joseph Yobo, Chelsea midfielder Jon Obi Mikel and a pair of free-scoring strikers in Everton's Yakubu Aiyegbeni and the pacy Martins, now with Wolfsburg after a mixed time in the Premiership with Newcastle. Yet, for all their obvious ability, Nigeria have often struggled to play as a team, relying instead on moments of individual brilliance to carry them through.

The tactics and selections of coach Shaibu Amodu, now in his fourth spell in charge of the national team, have also come under fire and there is a growing movement in Nigeria to have him replaced before the finals.

Such rumblings behind the scenes will clearly not help the Super Eagles' preparations for the tournament, but as long as the in-fighting does not get out of hand Nigeria could go far.

> "Nigeria don't fear any team but we know that it is not going to be an easy group."
>
> Nigeria coach Shaibu Amodu

NIGERIA AT THE WORLD CUP

• Nigeria reached their first World Cup in 1994 and, to the surprise of many, performed extremely well in the finals in the USA. Victories against Bulgaria and Greece ensured that the Super Eagles would top their group, and in the last 16 they came within a whisker of knocking out Italy before two Roberto Baggio goals condemned them to a 2-1 defeat after extra-time.

• **The Africans also topped their group at the 1998 tournament in France, this time thanks to victories over Spain and Bulgaria. However, an insipid display against Denmark in the last 16 saw them slump to a comprehensive 4-1 defeat.**

• Nigeria last reached the finals in 2002, but this time gave their fans little to cheer about. After disappointing defeats against Argentina and Sweden the Super Eagles did at least manage to hold England to a 0-0 draw, but one point from three games was a poor return for a team who had been tipped by some pundits as possible contenders before the tournament started.

PREVIOUS TOURNAMENTS

1930 Did not enter	1962 Did not qualify	1986 Did not qualify
1934 Did not enter	1966 Withdrew	1990 Did not qualify
1938 Did not enter	1970 Did not qualify	1994 Round 2
1950 Did not enter	1974 Did not qualify	1998 Round 2
1954 Did not enter	1978 Did not qualify	2002 Round 1
1958 Did not enter	1982 Did not qualify	2006 Did not qualify

KEY PLAYER:
YAKUBU AIYEGBENI

Along with his sidekick Obafemi Martins, Yakubu Aiyegbeni will form one of the most prolific striking partnerships at the World Cup. Yakubu himself has a strike rate approaching a goal every two games in his nearly 50 appearances for his country, and his pace, power and deadly shooting ability will be vital to his team's chances in South Africa.

Domestically, Yakubu has become the highest-scoring African player in Premiership history since first arriving at Portsmouth from Maccabi Haifa in 2002. He moved on to Middlesbrough in 2005 and helped the Teesiders reach the UEFA Cup final the following year before signing for Everton in 2007 for £11.25 million. His goals have made him a firm favourite at Goodison Park, which regularly rocks to the terrace chant 'Feed the Yak...and he will score!'.

SOUTH KOREA

South Korea have the best World Cup pedigree of any Asian country, famously reaching the semi-finals on home soil in 2002 when they were urged on by a huge army of red-clad supporters known as 'The Red Devils'. It would, though, be a major surprise if they did anywhere near as well this time around.

That is not to say, however, that South Korea's chances should be entirely discounted. For a start, they showed some impressive form en route to South Africa, remaining undefeated in 14 qualifying matches and conceding just seven goals in the process. Their success was based on a strong team ethic, good organisation and boundless drive and energy, and these qualities will serve them well once the tournament proper starts.

> **"To reach the round of 16 we must get a victory and two draws or two victories. There are no easy teams."**
>
> South Korea coach
> Huh Jung-Moo

Skipper Park Ji-Sung of Man Utd is easily their most famous player, but South Korea have a number of other talented performers. These include Monaco striker Park Chu-Young, Celtic's new midfielder Ki Sung-Yong and Bolton winger Lee Chung Yong, who revels in the nickname 'The Blue Dragon'. In Huh Jung-Moo, meanwhile, they have an experienced manager who has coached the national team twice before and is known to fans as 'Jindo Dog', after a popular breed of Korean dog known for its unwavering loyalty and bravery. His third spell in charge has been particularly noteworthy, with South Korea enjoying an incredible 27-game unbeaten run which only ended when they lost to Serbia at Craven Cottage in November 2009.

Well-drilled, committed and enthusiastic, South Korea will fight to the end but they might struggle in defence, where their lack of height could be exploited by taller and stronger opponents. Bearing in mind these shortcomings and the tough group they find themselves in their chances of reaching the last 16 must be rated as slim.

SOUTH KOREA AT THE WORLD CUP

• South Korea first competed at the World Cup in 1954 in Switzerland. In their first match they were thrashed 9-0 by Hungary – at the time the heaviest defeat in the tournament's history. They did slightly better in their second game, only losing 7-0 to Turkey.

• Hosting the tournament with Japan in 2002, South Korea finally gained their first win at the finals when they beat Poland 2-0. A goal by Park Ji-Sung enabled them to beat Portugal and top their group, before they sensationally defeated Italy 2-1 in the last 16. South Korea's winner was scored by Ahn Jung-Hwan but the next day he was unceremoniously sacked by his Italian club, Perugia. "I have no intention of paying a salary to someone who has ruined Italian football," said the club's president, Luciano Gaucci. Italy also felt they were cheated by some bizarre refereeing decision but it mattered not a jot to Guus Hiddink and his team.

• In the quarter-finals South Korea beat Spain 5-3 on penalties, but their luck ran out in the last four when they lost 1-0 to Germany.

• With six consecutive appearances at the finals South Korea are the most successful Asian country in World Cup history.

PREVIOUS TOURNAMENTS

1930 Did not enter	1962 Did not qualify	1986 Round 1
1934 Did not enter	1966 Did not enter	1990 Round 1
1938 Did not enter	1970 Did not qualify	1994 Round 1
1950 Did not enter	1974 Did not qualify	1998 Round 1
1954 Round 1	1978 Did not qualify	2002 Fourth place
1958 Entry not accepted	1982 Did not qualify	2006 Round 1

KEY PLAYER:
PARK JI-SUNG

An energetic performer either on the wing or in central midfield, South Korea captain Park Ji-Sung is the most popular sportsman in his country. He rose to prominence at the 2002 World Cup when, against the odds, South Korea reached the semi-finals before bowing out to Germany. Now fast approaching 100 caps, Park Ji-Sung also starred at the 2006 finals, scoring in his side's victory over Togo.

Park began his club career with Japanese outfit Kyoto Purple Sanga, before following his former national manager Guus Hiddink to PSV in 2003. Two years later he moved on to Manchester United, where he has become a valuable member of Sir Alex Ferguson's squad without quite cementing a regular first-team place. Nevertheless he has won numerous honours at Old Trafford, and in 2009 became the first Asian player to appear in the Champions League final.

GREECE

Greece's World Cup record is so poor that some might wonder if it is even worth them packing their suitcases for South Africa. However, it would be foolish to write them off completely, particularly when you remember that just six years ago the Greeks shocked the football world by winning the European Championships in Portugal.

The mastermind of that unexpected triumph was veteran German coach Otto Rehhagel, and the wily 71-year-old is still in charge of his adopted country. His team includes a core of heroes from the Euro 2004 tournament, sprinkled with a handful of younger players who have emerged in the ensuing years. One of the latter is Panathinaikos goalkeeper Alexandros Tzorvas, who performed brilliantly in the two-legged play-off victory against Ukraine that booked the Greeks' passage to South Africa. The defence is marshalled by two experienced campaigners in Liverpool's Sotirios Kyrgiakos and

> ## "Our football would be more attractive if we had Kaka, Messi and Xavi in our team."
>
> **Even Greece coach Otto Rehhagel accepts that his side are dull to watch**

Panathinaikos' Gioukas Seitoridis, while the midfield features two more players from Panathinaikos in the form of captain Giorgos Karagounis and the hard-working Kostas Katsouranis. In attack the Greeks rely heavily on Theofanis Gekas, the Bayer Leverkusen striker scoring half of his team's 20 goals in their qualifying group. Gekas will probably be supported by Celtic's Giorgos Samaras and Panathinaikos' Dimitrios Salpigidis, the scorer of the winning goal against Ukraine, although the pair will be under strict orders to drop into midfield as soon as possession is lost, turning Greece's 4-3-3 system into an ultra-defensive 4-5-1.

Well-drilled by Rehhagel, Greece are a solid, workmanlike side who will seek to sneak a goal on the counter-attack or from a set piece. They won't win any plaudits for artistic impression, but their cautious approach works well for them and they will be hard to beat.

GREECE AT THE WORLD CUP

• Expectations were high when Greece qualified for the World Cup for the first time in 1994. The team had topped their qualifying group with six wins and two draws from their eight games, raising hopes that the Greeks would prove a powerful force at the finals.

• **Those hopes, though, were quickly shattered when Greece were** trounced 4-0 in their first match by Argentina. The legendary Diego Maradona scored his last goal for his country in this game before later being banned from the rest of the competition after failing a drugs test.

• Greece's tournament, meanwhile, went from bad to worse as they lost 4-0 again, this time to Bulgaria, and then went down 2-0 to Nigeria. No points, no goals and ten conceded – the Greeks' abysmal record was one of the worst in World Cup history.

• **At least the misery was shared around: coach Alketas Panagoulius used all 22 of his players, including all three goalkeepers, in the three matches the team played.**

PREVIOUS TOURNAMENTS

1930 Did not enter	1962 Did not qualify	1986 Did not qualify
1934 Withdrew	1966 Did not qualify	1990 Did not qualify
1938 Did not qualify	1970 Did not qualify	1994 Round 1
1950 Did not enter	1974 Did not qualify	1998 Did not qualify
1954 Did not qualify	1978 Did not qualify	2002 Did not qualify
1958 Did not qualify	1982 Did not qualify	2006 Did not qualify

KEY PLAYER:
GIORGOS KARAGOUNIS

Greece captain Giorgos Karagounis will be 33 when the first ball is kicked in South Africa, but it is a mark of his importance to his side that he will still be the first name on coach Otto Rehhagel's teamsheet. A busy, tactically astute midfielder, Karagounis passes the ball well and, although not a prolific scorer, can shoot powerfully from distance.

Now approaching 100 caps for his country, Karagounis made his international debut against El Salvador way back in 1999. Five years later he starred at Euro 2004, scoring the first goal of the tournament against hosts Portugal with a long-range strike, although he missed the final against the same team through suspension. At club level, Karagounis is in his third spell with Panathinaikos, having previously played for European giants Inter Milan and Benfica.

ENGLAND

After plumbing the depths during the hapless reign of Steve McClaren, England have been revitalised under Italian manager Fabio Capello. The Three Lions will go to South Africa in confident mood and, as long as their key players stay fit, have a realistic chance of adding to their famous World Cup triumph in 1966.

ENGLAND v CROATIA
9 September 2009 WEMBLEY STADIUM

England swept through their qualifying group in fine style, winning nine out of ten matches and scoring 34 goals – the best total in the European zone. Moreover, some of their football was exhilarating, not least in the 5-1 thrashing of Croatia at Wembley which booked England's place at the finals.

> **"Every opponent will be strong because when you play in the World Cup, every game is not easy."**
> England coach
> Fabio Capello

Striker Wayne Rooney was the team's best player during the qualifiers, but the midfield trio of Steven Gerrard, Frank Lampard and Gareth Barry were also hugely impressive, while skipper John Terry and left-back Ashley Cole were the stand-out performers in defence.

Capello can rely on these six players in South Africa, but other areas of his line-up will give him more headaches. For a start, England lack a first-class goalkeeper, with current incumbent Robert Green seemingly as prone to catastrophic errors as his predecessor, David James. There are concerns too in the back four, with doubts over the fitness of centre-back Rio Ferdinand and the defensive capabilities of right-back Glen Johnson. Perhaps Capello's biggest dilemma, though, is who to play alongside the brilliant Rooney. The bustling Emile Heskey has long been his first choice, but has a poor scoring record at international level and, worryingly, is not even a regular starter for his club, Aston Villa.

If Capello can fix these various problems then England could go all the way. If not, then the Three Lions' roar may not last long once the knock-out stage begins.

THE GAFFER: FABIO CAPELLO

A shrewd tactician with a wealth of experience at the top level in Italy and Spain, Fabio Capello has transformed England's fortunes since taking the toughest job in football in January 2008. He inherited a squad low on confidence after England's failure to qualify for Euro 2008, but that soon changed as his new charges went on a magnificent run of eight straight World Cup victories – England's best ever start to a qualifying campaign.

A former Italian international striker who played for Roma, Juventus and AC Milan, Capello has a hugely impressive managerial CV. With AC Milan in the early 1990s he won the league title in four out of five seasons, and also led the rossoneri to a famous Champions League final victory over Barcelona in 1994. Further titles followed at Real Madrid in 1997, Roma in 2001 and Juventus in 2005 and 2006 (although the Turin club were later striped of these honours for their involvement in a match-fixing scandal). In 2006 Capello returned to Madrid, where his squad included England star David Beckham, and guided the Spanish giants to yet another title the following year.

KEY PLAYER:
WAYNE ROONEY

A genuine matchwinner who can change the course of a game in an instant, Wayne Rooney is vital to England's World Cup hopes. The Manchester United striker was in sparkling form during the qualifiers, scoring nine goals – an England record for a qualifying campaign – and will be one of the favourites for the Golden Boot in South Africa.

Now aged 24, Rooney was just 17 when he made his England debut against Australia in February 2003. Later that year he become his country's youngest ever scorer, but his biggest impact came at Euro 2004 when then England manager, Sven Goran Eriksson, famously compared Rooney to the young Pele. The 2006 World Cup was a less happy tournament for the Liverpool-born player: a pre-finals injury blunted his sharpness and he was sent off in the quarter-final defeat by Portugal for a petulant stamp.

Fabio Capello will be praying that Rooney's fuse does not blow again this summer, because if England were to lose their talismanic striker their chances of bringing the World Cup home would rapidly dwindle.

ONE TO WATCH: JERMAIN DEFOE

If England boss Fabio Capello selects his World Cup team on form rather than reputation then Tottenham's Jermain Defoe will be a shoe-in to partner Wayne Rooney in attack. The London-born striker enjoyed a fantastic campaign in 2009/10, equalling a longstanding Premiership individual scoring record when he bagged five goals in Spurs' 9-1 demolition of Wigan in November 2009.

Defoe began his career with West Ham, where his ability to hit the target from even the tightest of angles marked him out as a future star. He joined Tottenham for £6 million in 2004 but, after slipping down the pecking order at White Hart Lane, moved on to Portsmouth in 2008. The following year he returned to Spurs, linking up with former West Ham and Pompey manager Harry Redknapp for a third time.

Defoe made his England debut as a sub in a friendly against Sweden in 2004. He was a surprise omission from his country's 2006 World Cup squad but his excellent goalscoring record in recent seasons has seen him emerge as a strong candidate to lead England's attack in South Africa.

TACTICS BOARD: FAB FORMATION

Under Fabio Capello England generally play a 4-4-2 system, although with two central midfielders sitting deep and Wayne Rooney floating around a central striker the formation also has elements of 4-2-3-1.

A main plank of England's strategy is to dominate possession in the middle third of the pitch, where Frank Lampard and Gareth Barry are both excellent passers of the ball. With Aaron Lennon flying down the right, Steven Gerrard making his trademark surging runs on the left and two attack-minded full-backs in Ashley Cole and Glen Johnson, Capello's team has good width and puts in more crosses than most international teams.

Alongside the irrepressible Rooney, Capello has a preference for the muscular and physically imposing Emile Heskey, ahead of the more prolific, but much slighter, Jermain Defoe. Another striking option, meanwhile, is Tottenham beanpole Peter Crouch, although he is more likely to feature as a sub.

ENGLAND AT THE WORLD CUP

• England, along with the other home countries, declined to enter the first three World Cups following a dispute with FIFA about payments to amateur players. When England did eventually make their debut in 1950 in Brazil they crashed out at the group stage after a shock 1-0 defeat to the USA. A number of newspapers thought the result was so unlikely when they received it that they assumed it was a mistake, and instead printed the score as England 10 USA 1.

• **After reaching the quarter-finals in 1954 and 1962, England won the tournament as hosts in 1966. Alf Ramsey's 'wingless wonders', as they were dubbed, beat West Germany 4-2 in the final at Wembley, centre forward Geoff Hurst scoring a famous hat-trick. His second goal, which gave England a crucial 3-2 lead in extra-time, hit the crossbar before bouncing down on (or, in English eyes, over) the line and was only awarded after the referee had consulted his linesman.**

• England's hopes of defending their trophy in Mexico in 1970 got off to a bad start when, en route to the finals, their World Cup-winning captain Bobby Moore was arrested in Colombia on a trumped-up charge of stealing a bracelet from a shop.

Bobby Moore holds the World Cup aloft at Wembley in 1966

Moore was released to play in the tournament, but England crashed out 3-2 to old rivals West Germany in the quarter-finals.

• **After failing to qualify for the finals in 1974 and 1978, England reached the second group stage in Spain in 1982 but were knocked out despite not losing a match and only conceding one goal in five games.**

• In 1986 England striker Gary Lineker won the Golden Boot but Bobby Robson's team were knocked out in the quarter-finals by Argentina. Diego Maradona was the man who broke English hearts, first with his notorious 'Hand of God' goal then with a brilliant individual

strike in a 2-1 win for the South Americans.

• **England made their best recent showing at the World Cup in 1990, when Robson's men reached the semi-finals after dramatic late wins against Belgium and Cameroon. Sadly, they lost on penalties to West Germany, defender Stuart Pearce and winger Chris Waddle both missing from the spot.**

• England have since lost two more shoot-outs: against Argentina in 1998, and against Portugal in 2006. In between, they were beaten 2-1 by Brazil in a 2002 quarter-final despite taking the lead through Michael Owen.

PREVIOUS TOURNAMENTS

1930 Did not enter	1962 Quarter-finals	1986 Quarter-finals
1934 Did not enter	1966 Winners	1990 Semi-finals
1938 Did not enter	1970 Quarter-finals	1994 Did not qualify
1950 Round 1	1974 Did not qualify	1998 Round 2
1954 Quarter-finals	1978 Did not qualify	2002 Quarter-finals
1958 Round 1	1982 Round 2	2006 Quarter-finals

USA

'Soccer', as the Americans call it, may not be the most popular sport in the USA but few could fault the national team's efforts to raise the game's profile in their homeland. This, after all, will be the USA's sixth consecutive appearance at the World Cup finals – a record that many football-obsessed nations, including group opponents England, are unable to match.

More significantly, perhaps, the USA will be one of the form teams at the finals in South Africa. They came through the qualifying process relatively easily, topping their group and booking their place at the summer party with a game to spare after a 3-2 victory over Honduras. But it was their performances at the 2009 Confederations Cup in South Africa that really marked them out as a side to watch. First, the USA beat Spain 2-0 in the semi-final, ending the European champions' record 35-match unbeaten run; then, they shocked Brazil by racing into a 2-0 half-time lead in the final before finally losing 3-2.

> **"We understand the responsibility we have every time we step on the field -for our fans, for our country."**
>
> USA coach
> Bob Bradley

Strangely, the USA's success has been achieved without a regular, settled side. Coach Bob Bradley used 43 players during the qualifiers and has tried out more than 70 since being appointed in January 2007.

In South Africa, though, he will rely on a core of experienced players who include Everton goalkeeper Tim Howard, skipper Carlos Bocanegra, formerly of Fulham but now with French side Rennes, West Ham full back Jonathan Spector, star player Landon Donovan and Fulham striker Clint Dempsey. There may also be a place for Bradley's son, Michael, a busy central midfielder who plays for Borussia Monchengladbach.

A well-organised, physically fit side who carry a goal threat, the USA have the capacity to surprise more renowned teams and could be an outside bet to reach the latter stages. At the very least, they will be favourites alongside England to emerge from Group C.

USA AT THE WORLD CUP

• The USA competed at the first World Cup in Argentina in 1930, reaching the semi-finals after 3-0 victories against Belgium and Paraguay. In the second of these matches Bert Patenaude scored all three of the USA's goals to claim the first ever hat-trick at the finals.

• **In 1950 the USA pulled off one of the biggest surprises in the history of the competition when they beat England 1-0 in Belo Horizonte, Brazil. Haitian-born striker Joe Gaetjens wrote himself into the history books by heading the winner.**

• The USA hosted the tournament in 1994 and reached the knock-out stage for the first time since 1930, thanks mainly to a 2-1 victory against Colombia. They were helped by an own goal by Colombian defender Andres Escobar, whose mistake later cost him his life when he was shot dead in his home country.

• **The USA failed to win a match on their last World Cup appearance in 2006, their only point coming in a creditable 1-1 draw with eventual champions Italy.**

PREVIOUS TOURNAMENTS

1930 Third place	1962 Did not qualify	1986 Did not qualify
1934 Round 1	1966 Did not qualify	1990 Round 1
1938 Withdrew	1970 Did not qualify	1994 Round 1
1950 Round 1	1974 Did not qualify	1998 Round 1
1954 Did not qualify	1978 Did not qualify	2002 Quarter-finals
1958 Did not qualify	1982 Did not qualify	2006 Round 1

KEY PLAYER:
LANDON DONOVAN

A danger to opposition defences whether playing as an attacking midfielder or a withdrawn striker, Landon Donovan is the USA's all-time leading scorer having notched more than 40 goals for his country since making his international debut in 2000. He first made a mark on the world stage when he was voted Best Young Player at the 2002 World Cup, a tournament at which the USA surpassed expectations by reaching the quarter-finals.

A graduate of the US Soccer Academy, Donovan started his club career with Bayer Leverkusen but soon returned to his homeland to play for San Jose Earthquakes, with whom he won two MLS Cups. Now with Los Angeles Galaxy (aside from a loan spell with Everton), he was voted USA national team Player of the Year in 2009, the sixth time he has won the award.

ALGERIA

Twenty-four years after their last appearance at the finals Algeria return to the world stage as the only representatives from north Africa. The Desert Foxes, or Les Fennecs as they are known by their fans, will be hoping to make up for lost time and will certainly fancy their chances of progressing from Group C along with hot favourites England.

If Algeria can reproduce the form they showed in qualifying then few would bet against them advancing to the second round. Their play-off victory against Egypt in the Sudanese capital of Khartoum was particularly impressive, Bochum defender Antar Yahia volleying home a superb winner from an acute angle to book his country's passage to South Africa and spark wild celebrations from Algiers to the Sahara desert.

> **"I think it's a difficult group and one that gives England and the USA an advantage."**
>
> Algeria coach
> Rabah Saadane

Yahia is a regular in a defence which also includes Rangers' Majid Bougherra and Portsmouth's Nadir Belhadj, although the pacy Pompey star is sometimes deployed as a wing-back in a 3-5-2 formation by Algeria's 63-year-old coach Rabah Saadane, who is currently in his fifth stint as national team manager. Yazid Mansouri, who had a brief spell at Coventry City in the 2003/04 season, is likely to fill a deep-lying midfield role, while alongside him the highly-rated Karim Ziani will be given greater licence to attack. Up front, Saadane will probably stick with veteran striker Rafik Saifi, and the 35-year-old may be partnered by lively Hull City forward Kamel Ghilas. Algeria's goalkeeper, meanwhile, is one Lounes Gaouaoui. His vowel-heavy surname may give TV commentators nightmares but the viewing millions around the globe will certainly enjoy watching him make the spectacular saves for which he is renowned.

Defensively sound, well-organised and tactically astute, Algeria will be no pushovers but a less than prolific strikeforce may prevent them from reaching the knock-out stages.

ALGERIA AT THE WORLD CUP

• In their first ever match at the World Cup in 1982 Algeria pulled off one of the biggest shocks in the tournament's history, beating West Germany 2-1 in Gijon, Spain. The winning goal was scored by Lakhdar Belloumi, African Footballer of the Year in 1981 and widely recognised as the best Algerian player ever.

• At the same tournament Algeria beat Chile 3-2 to give themselves a good opportunity of becoming the first African country to progress beyond the group stages. However, the following day West Germany defeated Austria 1-0, a result which ensured that both countries would reach the next round at the expense of Algeria on goal difference.

• The north Africans protested that their two rivals had connived in producing a result that suited both teams, and the unusually slow tempo of the game certainly suggested some sort of agreement had been struck. FIFA, though, waved away Algeria's complaints although it did rule that the last two matches in a group should be played at the same time at future World Cups.

PREVIOUS TOURNAMENTS

1930 Did not enter	1962 Did not enter	1986 Round 1
1934 Did not enter	1966 Withdrew	1990 Did not qualify
1938 Did not enter	1970 Did not qualify	1994 Did not qualify
1950 Did not enter	1974 Did not qualify	1998 Did not qualify
1954 Did not enter	1978 Did not qualify	2002 Did not qualify
1958 Did not enter	1982 Round 1	2006 Did not qualify

KEY PLAYER:
KARIM ZIANI

A skilful midfielder who possesses quick feet and an eye for the killer pass, 27-year-old Karim Ziani plays for Wolfsburg in the Bundesliga. Prior to joining the German outfit in the summer of 2009, Ziani had spent all of his professional career in France, starting out with Troyes before spells with Lorient, Sochaux and Marseille.

Ziani made his debut for Algeria in 2003 and the following year performed magnificently for the Desert Foxes at the African Nations Cup in Tunisia. Although the finals ended disappointingly for Algeria when they were knocked out in the quarter-finals by Morocco, Ziani was voted the best player in his position in the tournament. Since then he has established himself as his country's most important player, his displays in the qualifying rounds being central to Algeria's success.

SLOVENIA

The smallest country at the finals, Slovenia caused the biggest shock in qualifying when they knocked out Russia in the play-offs to book their place in South Africa. A hard-working, well-organised side with a touch of flair they have been rewarded with a decent draw and will fancy their chances of progressing to the knock-out stage for the first time in their history.

That victory over Russia was probably the greatest day in Slovenia's football history – although this is a period which only stretches back to 1992, the year after the country split from the former Yugoslavia. It came courtesy of a goal by Bochum striker Zlatko Dedic in Maribor, which was enough to put Slovenia through on the away goals rule after they had lost 2-1 in Moscow four days earlier.

> **"Slovenia is small but with great, great heart and this is one of the biggest plusses for our team."**
>
> Slovenia coach
> Matjaz Kek

The platform for Slovenia's success was provided by a stingy defence which only conceded four goals in 10 group games – a record only bettered by Holland. The outstanding performer in that rearguard is Udinese goalkeeper Samir Handanovic who, despite being aged just 25, has already won nearly 40 caps. In front of him, the back four includes Grenoble's Bostjan Cesar, who enjoyed a loan spell with West Brom in 2007/08.

The most familiar name to England fans, though, is a current Baggies player, Robert Koren. A midfielder with a neat touch, good passing skills and excellent vision, Koren is the playmaker in coach Matjaz Kek's side, and his performances will be crucial to Slovenia's chances. In attack, Kek usually employs two strikers in a 4-4-2 formation, the most likely starters being Dedic and the gangly Milivoje Novakovic, a prolific scorer in the Bundesliga with Cologne.

As Russia found to their cost, Slovenia are a difficult side to break down and they will provide awkward opposition at the finals.

SLOVENIA AT THE WORLD CUP

• Slovenia have only appeared at the finals once before. That was in 2002 when, after finishing second behind Russia in their qualifying group, they reached Japan and Korea thanks to a play-off victory against Romania.

• **Slovenia had not lost a single one of their 12 qualifying matches, but their good form deserted them at the finals. In their first game against Spain they went down to a 3-1 defeat, Sebastjan Cimirotic grabbing a consolation goal. In the dressing room afterwards a clash between star player Zlatko Zahovic** and manager Srecko Katanec led to the Benfica forward being sent home from the Far East.

• Without the talismanic Zahovic, Slovenia slumped to a 1-0 defeat to South Africa and then lost 3-1 to Paraguay despite leading at half-time against 10 men. All in all, it had been a World Cup debut to forget.

• Slovenia failed to make it the 2006 finals in Germany but they did beat Italy 1-0 at home in their qualifying group – the only defeat suffered by the Italians on their way to winning the tournament.

PREVIOUS TOURNAMENTS

1930-1990 Did not enter (was part of Yugoslavia)
1994 Did not enter
1998 Did not qualify
2002 Round 1
2006 Did not qualify

KEY PLAYER:
MILIVOJE NOVAKOVIC

Slovenia's leading scorer in qualifying with five goals, 30-year-old Milivoje Novakovic will be his country's main attacking threat in South Africa. The 6 ft 4 in striker presents an obvious danger in the air but, rather like England's Peter Crouch, has good skills on the ground and is much more than a mere lofty targetman.

Novakovic was something of a late developer, plying his trade in the Austrian lower leagues before finally making his mark at Litex Lovech, with whom he topped the Bulgarian scoring charts in 2006. A move to Cologne followed, and two years later Novakovic's 20 goals powered the Germans to promotion. The following season he added another 16 in the Bundesliga to gain a reputation as one of the league's top strikers.

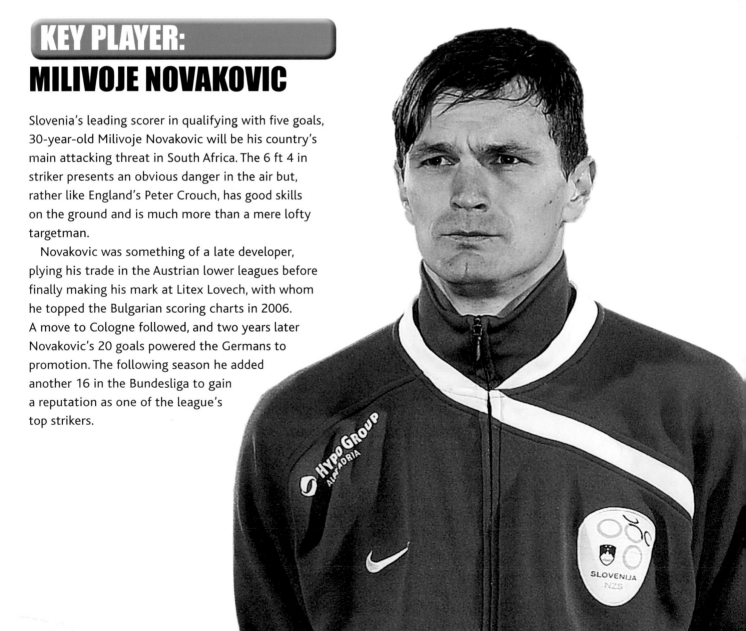

GERMANY

Hosts at the last World Cup in 2006, Germany will go to the tournament in South Africa hoping to feature in a record eighth final. Or should that be 'expecting to feature'? Quarter-finalists at the very least in each of the 14 World Cups, the Germans have a back catalogue of consistent achievement that simply inspires confidence.

The bigger the game, the better Germany play. Even in the qualifiers this trait was very much to the fore, as the Germans won both their two crucial head-to-heads with main rivals Russia to top their group. Their victory in Moscow was particularly impressive, striker Miroslav Klose getting the only goal of the game to clinch his team's place in South Africa.

> "There is a good chance we will reach the final again."
>
> Germany captain Michael Ballack

Germany's traditional strengths are their fitness, organisation and team spirit. Those qualities will again be in evidence this summer but this could be a slightly less methodical German team than normal if coach Joachim Low selects rising star Mesut Ozil, a gifted midfielder of Turkish heritage who demolished England almost single-handedly in the 2009 Under-21 European Championship final.

Whether Ozil starts or not, Germany will carry a goal threat in veteran Bayern Munich striker Miroslav Klose, the Golden Boot winner in 2006, and Cologne's Lukas Podolski. In midfield, meanwhile, the vastly experienced Michael Ballack is a hugely influential figure with a tremendous goalscoring record at international level. Behind him, six foot six inch centre-half Per Mertesacker is the dominant figure in defence alongside Bayer Leverkusen's highly-rated goalkeeper, Rene Adler.

Given their outstanding World Cup record, it would seem foolish to bet against Germany. However, they are possibly not quite as strong as in previous tournaments, and may find yet another appearance in the final just beyond them.

THE GAFFER: JOACHIM LOW

Germany coach Joachim Low has been associated with the national team since 2004, when he was appointed as Jurgen Klinsmann's assistant. Two years later the pair led Germany to the semi-finals of the World Cup, with the tactically astute Low being given much credit for implementing Klinsmann's attacking philosophy. When Klinsmann declined to renew his contract after the end of the tournament, Low stepped up to take the top job.

He made the best ever start of a German national team coach, guiding his side to five straight wins. Low then masterminded Germany's route to the final of Euro 2008, although defeat by Spain meant he failed to get his hands on the trophy. Still, the campaign improved his reputation, largely ending doubts about whether he had the necessary charisma to be a successful number one.

A journeyman midfielder in his playing career with Freiburg, Eintracht Frankfurt and Karlsruher, Low began his management career with Stuttgart, leading them to the final of the European Cup Winners' Cup in 1998. He later managed in Turkey and Austria, leading Tirol Innsbruck to the league title in 2002.

KEY PLAYER:
MICHAEL BALLACK

An attacking midfielder who is particularly strong in the air, Germany captain Michael Ballack is still a central figure for his country more than a decade after he first appeared on the international scene.

Three years after making his debut for Germany, Ballack scored the goal against hosts South Korea that took his side through to the 2002 World Cup final, although he was suspended for the subsequent defeat by Brazil. Six years later he skippered his country to the final of Euro 2008, but again just missed out on a top honour after Germany lost to Spain.

In all likelihood, the World Cup in South Africa represents the last chance of glory for the 33-year-old at international level, but if Ballack fails to collect the biggest prize of all he can console himself by counting his numerous domestic honours. These include three Bundesliga and German Cup doubles with Bayern Munich, and the FA and Carling Cups with Chelsea, who he joined on a free transfer from Bayern in the summer of 2006.

ONE TO WATCH: LUKAS PODOLSKI

Since making his international debut in 2004 Lukas Podolski has gained a reputation as one of the most prolific strikers in world football. One country's gain is very much another's loss in his case, because Podolski was actually born in Poland and only moved to Germany with his parents, both Poles themselves, when he was two years old.

As a teenager Podolski harboured dreams of running out in the red and white of Poland but he was eventually persuaded to represent his adopted country. He made his debut for Germany in 2004 but only really rose to prominence at the 2006 World Cup, when he scored three goals to finish joint second behind team-mate Miroslav Klose in the race for the Golden Boot. He enjoyed another good tournament at Euro 2008, where his three goals – including two in a defeat of Poland, which he refused to celebrate – helped Germany reach the final.

At club level, Podolski left yo-yo club Cologne after their relegation in 2006, signing for Bayern Munich for around £8 million. However, after three mixed years with the Bundesliga giants, he returned to Cologne in 2009.

TACTICS BOARD:
OZIL THE KEY MAN

The emergence of 21-year-old playmaker Mesut Ozil may tempt Germany coach Joachim Low to plump for a 4-2-3-1 system in South Africa. The Werder Bremen starlet only has a handful of caps but has impressed in his outings to date, and has the necessary skill and creativity to pull the strings behind targetman Miroslav Klose. In this formation Lukas Podolski and Bastian Schweinsteiger would provide support for Klose from the flanks, with Michael Ballack and Bayer Leverkusen's Simon Rolfes sitting deeper in midfield.

The alternative would be to push Podolski up front with Klose in a 4-4-2, but few international teams play with two strikers these days as it tends to leave them outnumbered in midfield. Whichever system Low opts for, left-back Phillip Lahm will need little encouragement to bomb forward while the likes of Ballack and towering centre-back Per Mertesacker pose a major threat at set-pieces.

GERMANY AT THE WORLD CUP

• Germany first competed at the World Cup in Italy in 1934. In a sign of things to come they did pretty well, reaching the semi-finals before losing 3-1 to Czechoslovakia in Rome.

• **After being excluded from the 1950 tournament by FIFA for starting World War II, the Germans returned in 1954 (as West Germany) and won their first trophy after coming from 2-0 down to beat Hungary 3-2 in the final in Berne. The result was a surprise as the brilliant Hungarians had earlier thrashed the Germans 8-3 in a group game.**

• West Germany reached the final again in 1966, but lost 4-2 at Wembley to hosts England after extra-time. To this day the Germans bitterly complain that England's controversial third goal did not actually cross the line.

• **They made up for that disappointment as hosts in 1974, however, beating Holland 2-1 in the final in Munich to claim their second World Cup. Germany's hero was prolific striker Gerd Muller who scored the winner after both teams had converted penalties.**

• West Germany reached the final for a fourth time in 1982 after beating

Lothar Matthaus and Rudi Voller celebrate success in 1990

France in the first ever World Cup shoot-out in the semi-final. Their luck ran out against Italy, though, who claimed the trophy with a 3-1 victory in Madrid.

• **Fours years later West Germany reached the final again, but went down to a Diego Maradona-inspired Argentina in a five-goal thriller in Mexico City.**

• The Germans made it three finals on the trot in 1990, their opponents once again being Argentina. Managed by the legendary Franz Beckenbauer, their World Cup-winning captain of 1974, the Germans got their revenge thanks to a late penalty by defender Andreas Brehme.

• **After shock quarter-final defeats**

to Bulgaria in 1994 and Croatia four years later, Germany reached **their seventh final in 2002. The Germans' star player up until that point had been goalkeeper Oliver Kahn, but his blunder gifted opponents Brazil their opening goal in the South Americans' 2-0 victory in Yokohama.**

• Germany hosted the tournament for a second time in 2006 and, coached by 1990 World Cup winner Jurgen Klinsmann, they seemed destined to reach a record eighth final until they lost 2-0 to eventual champions Italy in the semi-finals. There was some consolation, though, for Germany striker Miroslav Klose who was the tournament's top scorer with five goals.

PREVIOUS TOURNAMENTS

1930 Did not enter	1962 Quarter-finals	1986 Runners-up
1934 Third place	1966 Runners-up	1990 Winners
1938 Round 1	1970 Third place	1994 Quarter-finals
1950 Banned	1974 Winners	1998 Quarter-finals
1954 Winners	1978 Round 1	2002 Runners-up
1958 Fourth place	1982 Runners-up	2006 Third place

* Competed as West Germany 1950-90

AUSTRALIA

Australia's line-up in South Africa will read almost like a Premiership Select XI, with the likes of Mark Schwarzer, Lucas Neill and Brett Emerton all well-known to followers of the English domestic game. And while the Socceroos' most famous player, Harry Kewell, now plays for Turkish giants Galatasaray his stints at Leeds and Liverpool are still fondly recalled by fans of those clubs.

Coach Pim Verbeek, though, will be a less familiar figure. A Dutchman, Verbeek was South Korea's assistant manager at the last two World Cups and his tournament know-how will prove an asset to a team which is defensively strong but lacking in attacking flair. Verbeek's cautious 4-2-3-1 system has been labelled 'boring' by the Australian media, but the simple truth is that the Socceroos don't have the striking talent to play a more adventurous formation.

With veteran centre forward Mark Viduka unlikely to figure, much speculation will surround who will fill his lone striker's boots. The most likely candidate is Joshua Kennedy, a six foot four inch giant currently playing in Japan with Nagoya Grampus. Dubbed 'Jesus' because of his long hair and straggly beard, Kennedy scored three goals during Australia's qualifying campaign and his towering presence could unsettle the Socceroos' three group opponents.

Certainly, Kennedy is a more likely starter than either Archie Thompson or Danny Allsopp, two Australian A-League strikers whose performances in a recent 0-0 draw against Indonesia were slammed by the straight-talking Verbeek as "absolutely hopeless". Whoever plays up front, though, goals could be in short supply for an Australian side which will be dogged, determined and difficult to break down, but may lack sufficient creativity and attacking prowess to match their achievement in 2006 when they reached the second round.

> "Germany's one of the best teams in the world – it's a great opponent for the first game."
>
> Australia coach Pim Verbeek

AUSTRALIA AT THE WORLD CUP

• Australia first played at the World Cup in 1974 in West Germany, but went home early after failing to score a single goal in their three group games. The Socceroos, though, did at least manage to pick up a point thanks to a 0-0 draw against Chile.

• Following a number of near misses, Australia reached the finals for a second time in 2006. After opening with a 3-1 victory over

Japan, the Aussies then lost to Brazil to leave them needing a point against Croatia to progress to the last 16. That's exactly what they got, too, thanks to Harry Kewell's late equaliser in a 2-2 draw which ended in bizarre circumstances when English referee Graham Poll only sent off Croatia's Josip Simunic after showing him three yellow cards

• Superbly organized by manager Guus Hiddink, Australia put up a brave fight in the next round against eventual winners Italy but were eventually beaten by a controversial last-minute Francesco Totti penalty.

• In a qualifier for the 2002 tournament Australia beat American Samoa 31-0, the biggest win in World Cup history.

PREVIOUS TOURNAMENTS

1930 Did not enter	1962 Did not enter	1986 Did not qualify
1934 Did not enter	1966 Did not qualify	1990 Did not qualify
1938 Did not enter	1970 Did not qualify	1994 Did not qualify
1950 Did not enter	1974 Round 1	1998 Did not qualify
1954 Did not enter	1978 Did not qualify	2002 Did not qualify
1958 Did not enter	1982 Did not qualify	2006 Round 2

KEY PLAYER:

TIM CAHILL

Everton midfielder Tim Cahill will be one of Australia's main attacking weapons in South Africa. His greatest strength is his heading ability which, allied to his talent for making perfectly timed runs into the opposition penalty area, has made him a consistent scorer for the Toffees in the Premiership.

He is also a regular on the scoresheet for his country, most notably coming off the bench against Japan at the last World Cup to net twice as the Socceroos fought back from a goal down to record an historic first victory at the finals.

"The whole of Australia can probably say exactly where they were when those two goals went in," Cahill later reflected. "For me, that's something I can share with every single Australian." No doubt he'll be hoping to share similar magical moments with the Aussie fans this summer.

SERBIA

Serbia are making their first appearance at the World Cup as an independent nation, having featured at the 2006 finals as Serbia & Montenegro and, previously, as part of Yugoslavia. The White Eagles, as they are known to their fans, will be determined to make a success of their debut and their form in qualifying suggests they could be a team to avoid.

To the surprise of many, Serbia finished above France in their group, condemning the 2006 runners-up to a tricky play-off with Ireland. The team's performances, not least the 5-0 drubbing of Romania in Belgrade that booked their place in South Africa, will have delighted Serbian coach Radomir Antic, a former Luton Town player who has managed both Real Madrid and Barcelona in his time.

Serbia, who generally line up in a 4-4-2 formation, are particularly strong in central defence where Manchester United stopper Nemanja Vidic and Chelsea hardman Branislav

> **"All our rivals are top quality teams, but I think we have realistic chance of reaching the last 16."**
> Serbia manager
> Radomir Antic

Ivanovic have a good understanding. Captain Dejan Stankovic is a classy performer in midfield, where he can count on excellent support from free-kick specialist Milan Javanovic, Serbia's top scorer in the qualifiers with five goals, and pacy CSKA Moscow wideman Milos Krasic. The attack, though, is less impressive, with Valencia targetman Nikola Zigic an inconsistent finisher and his partner, Marko Pantelic of Ajax, more likely to provide assists than goals. Still, the team as a whole has not found goals hard to come by thanks to regular contributions from the midfield and Ivanovic, who is a real danger at set pieces.

A tough, solid outfit, Serbia should do well at the finals and could certainly reach the last 16, where they might well face England. However, the lack of a world-class striker means they could struggle to get any further in the competition.

SERBIA AT THE WORLD CUP

• In their former guise as Yugoslavia, the team reached the semi-finals of the first World Cup only to crash 6-1 to hosts and eventual winners Uruguay – the joint heaviest ever defeat at that advanced stage of the competition.

• **Yugoslavia beat West Germany to reach the semi-finals again in 1962 in Chile, but came a cropper against Czechoslovakia who ran out** 3-1 winners.

• Banned from entering the World Cup in 1994 because of the civil wars in the former Yugoslavia, Serbia had to wait until 2006 before competing at the finals. After conceding just one goal in ten qualifiers – the best record in the whole of Europe – the Serbs travelled to Germany in confident mood.

• **However, their fabled defence disintegrated on the world stage in embarrassing fashion. After a narrow 1-0 defeat by Holland, the Serbs were crushed 6-0 by Argentina and finished a miserable campaign bottom of their group after throwing away a 2-0 lead to lose 3-2 to the Ivory Coast in their final match.**

PREVIOUS TOURNAMENTS

1930 Fourth place	1962 Fourth place	1986 Did not qualify
1934 Did not qualify	1966 Did not qualify	1990 Quarter-finals
1938 Did not qualify	1970 Did not qualify	1994 Banned
1950 Round 1	1974 Round 2	1998 Did not qualify
1954 Quarter-finals	1978 Did not qualify	2002 Did not qualify
1958 Quarter-finals	1982 Round 1	2006 Round 1

* Competed as Yugoslavia (1930-2002) and as Serbia & Montenegro (2006)

KEY PLAYER:
DEJAN STANKOVIC

Now 31, Dejan Stankovic is a gifted midfielder who has played at the top level in Italy for more than a decade after starting out with his local club, Red Star Belgrade. His powerful shooting and inventive passing soon alerted scouts from the top European sides, and in 1998 Stankovic joined Lazio. The following year he helped the Romans win the last ever edition of the Cup Winners' Cup, and in 2000 he played an instrumental role in the club's second ever Serie A title triumph. Four years later Stankovic moved to Inter Milan, with whom he has since won four more Scudetto titles.

First capped against South Korea in 1998, Stankovic is now approaching 90 caps for his country. He skippered Serbia (& Montenegro) at the World Cup in 2006 and will wear the armband again in South Africa.

GROUP D

GHANA

It might be tempting fate to say so, but everything is set up for Ghana to enjoy an excellent World Cup. Confidence in the Black Stars' camp is sky-high after they cruised through their qualifying group, the squad has a core of talented players at the height of their powers and, like all the African nations, Ghana will receive strong support at the finals.

The team's great strength is in midfield, where the surging runs of Chelsea's Michael Essien are complemented by the industry of captain Stephen Appiah, now with Bologna after spending nearly a year without a club, and the probing passes of Inter Milan's Sulley Muntari. The Black Stars' defence is, perhaps, not quite as strong but features steady performers in Wigan reserve goalkeeper Richard Kingson and Fulham's tough-tackling full-back John Pantsil. Up front, Serbian coach Milovan Rajevac usually opts for Rennes striker Asamoah Gyan and NAC Breda's Matthew Amoah,

> "It was a fantastic feeling to be the first African country to qualify for the first World Cup to be staged in Africa."
>
> Ghana's star player, Michael Essien

both of whom have a decent scoring record at international level.

A powerful side with a touch of flair, Ghana should be able to navigate their way through the group stages, although they could have wished for easier opponents than Germany, Serbia and Australia. Their problems may come later in the competition, particularly if any of their key players pick up injuries or suspensions before the knock-out phase. That, in a nutshell, was the story of Ghana's first World Cup in 2006. Without the suspended Essien they crashed to a 3-0 defeat against Brazil in the last 16, an inept offside trap also contributing to their downfall.

Presumably, the Black Stars will have learned from that chastening experience and will be less tactically naïve this time around. If that proves to be the case, another last 16 appearance – and a possible meeting with England – is well within their reach.

GHANA AT THE WORLD CUP

• Ghana made their World Cup debut in Germany in 2006, performing beyond expectations to become the only African side to reach the second round.

• The Black Stars began their campaign with a 2-0 defeat at the hands of eventual champions Italy, but bounced back in their second match to beat the Czech Republic by the same score. Requiring a victory against the USA to be certain of reaching the knock-out stages, Ghana won 2-1 with captain Stephen Appiah slotting home the decisive goal from the penalty spot on the stroke of half-time.

• That's as good as it got for Ghana, who were beaten 3-0 by Brazil in the last 16. When Ronaldo opened the scoring for the South Americans after just five minutes of the match he took his World Cup tally to 15 goals, a record for the tournament.

• The Ghanaians were the youngest side at the 2006 finals, with an average age of 23 years and 352 days. Despite lacking experience they did their country proud and were quite rightly given a heroes' reception when they returned home.

PREVIOUS TOURNAMENTS

1930 Did not enter	1962 Did not qualify	1986 Did not qualify
1934 Did not enter	1966 Withdrew	1990 Did not qualify
1938 Did not enter	1970 Did not qualify	1994 Did not qualify
1950 Did not enter	1974 Did not qualify	1998 Did not qualify
1954 Did not enter	1978 Did not qualify	2002 Did not qualify
1958 Did not enter	1982 Withdrew	2006 Round 2

KEY PLAYER:
MICHAEL ESSIEN

Dubbed 'The Bison' for his powerhouse performances for Chelsea and Ghana, Michael Essien is one of the best midfielders in the world. A magnificent competitor who uses the ball well, Essien is also capable of scoring from distance and his all-action displays have earned him many admirers. "Essien is a great player," his former Chelsea manager Jose Mourinho once said. "He can play every position in midfield. He controls the pace of the game, fast or slow."

Perhaps Essien's only weakness is a tendency to throw himself into tackles which he has little chance of winning, with the result that he has picked up more than his fair share of yellow cards and suspensions. Ghana fans will be praying he has no such problems in South Africa because without him the Black Lions are not the same team.

NETHERLANDS

For nearly four decades the Netherlands' role at the finals has been that of the great entertainers who always fall just short of landing the great prize. As the tournament in South Africa approaches ever nearer it's safe to assume that their huge army of orange-clad fans will all be asking the same question: namely, can the Dutch finally turn their undoubted talent into genuine achievement?

Certainly, the signs in the Netherlands' qualifying campaign were positive. The Dutch cruised through their group with a 100 per cent record, making light work of Norway, Scotland, Macedonia and Iceland. True, the opposition wasn't up to much but, as the old saying goes, you can only beat what is put in front you – and that's precisely what the Oranje did, conceding just two goals along the way.

> **"We should be able to beat any opponent if we want to win the World Cup."**
>
> Netherlands coach
> Bert van Marwijk

Ironically, given that impressive statistic, the Netherlands' defence is widely considered to be the weakest part of their team. In goal, Ajax's Maarten Stekelenburg lacks the experience and presence of his predecessor, Edwin van der Sar, while there are concerns that captain Giovanni van Bronckurst and central defender Andre Ooijer, who will both be 35 when the World Cup starts, are now some way past their best.

Still, the Netherlands have a lot of quality elsewhere, no more so than in attack where Arsenal's Robin van Persie, former Chelsea winger Arjen Robben and Inter Milan's Wesley Sneijder are as good a front trio as any team can boast.

If those three perform as they can then the Netherlands should have few problems reaching the quarter-finals at the very least. Coach Bert van Marwijk, a former manager of Feyenoord, is certainly bullish about his team's chances, saying, "We know that if we have our strongest team and everyone is in form, we can beat everyone."

THE GAFFER: BERT VAN MARWIJK

Bert van Marwijk was not a universally popular choice to succeed Marco van Basten as the Netherlands coach in 2008, mainly because his Feyenoord side had failed to challenge for the Dutch title during his two spells with the club. However, the silver-haired 57-year-old won over many of his detractors after the Netherlands qualified for South Africa in impressive style.

An attacking midfielder in his playing days, Van Marwijk turned out for Go Ahead Eagles, AZ Alkmaar and MVV Maastricht, making a single appearance for his country in 1975. His best achievement as a coach was winning the UEFA Cup with Feyenoord in 2002, and he also led the Rotterdam club to a Dutch Cup success in 2008. In between, he spent two-and-a-half undistinguished years with Borussia Dortmund, getting the sack after failing to lift the Bundesliga outfit beyond mid-table mediocrity.

Van Marwijk says he does not 'believe in systems', preferring instead to encourage his midfielders and strikers to interchange positions. Something of an unknown quantity outside his native Netherlands, he once summed up his approach to the game by saying, "I like attacking football. But I also like winning."

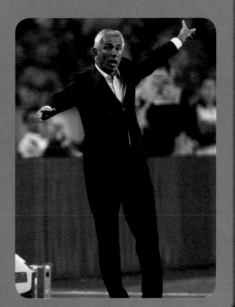

KEY PLAYER:
WESLEY SNEIJDER

An intelligent player who likes to drop into the spaces between midfield and attack where he can either thread the ball through to a striker or try his luck from distance, Wesley Sneijder is one of the most technically gifted players in the Dutch team.

A product of the famous Ajax youth system, Sneijder came through the ranks to become a key performer for the Amsterdam side before joining Real Madrid for around £20 million in 2007. He helped the Spanish giants win La Liga in his first season but subsequently dropped out of favour at the Bernabeu and left for Inter Milan in 2009. He starred in a 4-0 rout of city rivals AC on his debut, and appears rejuvenated since moving to Italy.

Sneijder's prodigious talent earned him an international call up against Portugal in 2003 when he was just 18. In the years since he has become a mainstay of the Dutch side, being particularly impressive at Euro 2008 where he was voted into the Team of the Tournament.

ONE TO WATCH: ROBIN VAN PERSIE

A superb striker of the ball particularly on his preferred left side, Robin Van Persie provides a cutting edge to the Netherlands' slick approach play. His recovery from a serious ankle injury, which ruled him out of much of the 2009/10 campaign, will be crucial if the Dutch are to fulfil their undoubted potential in South Africa.

The son of two artists, Van Persie began his career with his local side, Feyenoord, making his first-team debut aged 17 in 2001 and winning the Dutch league's Best Young Talent award at the end of his first season. A UEFA Cup winner the following year, he moved to Arsenal in 2004 in a £2.75 million deal. In his first season with the Gunners he helped them win the FA Cup, but medals have been harder to come by in the years since that first triumph.

He made his debut for Netherlands in a World Cup qualifier against Romania in 2005, and played in all four of his country's games at the finals in Germany the next year, scoring with a magnificent free-kick against Ivory Coast.

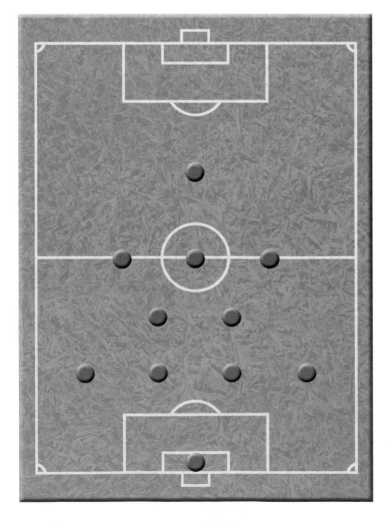

TACTICS BOARD:
ORANGE FAB FOUR

Usually one of the most attractive sides to watch at the World Cup, the Netherlands play a 4-2-3-1 system that gives their attacking players every opportunity to express themselves in the final third.

Taking their cue from past Dutch sides, particularly the early 1970s pioneers of 'Total Football', the front four like to swap positions on a regular basis, although Robin van Persie is the most likely to turn up at the point of the attack. He is supported by a trio who offer very different qualities: Bayern Munich's Arjen Robben, a skilful, turbo-charged winger; Wesley Sneijder, a subtle, two-footed playmaker; and, last but not least, Liverpool's Dirk Kuyt, a hard-working terrier with a poacher's nose for goal.

Behind this foursome, Manchester City's Nigel de Jong and Bayern Munich's Mark van Bommel, are a pair of tough-tackling midfielders who provide protection for a defence which appears to be the Netherlands' main weak point.

THE NETHERLANDS AT THE WORLD CUP

The great Johan Cruyff in action in 1974

legendary names such as Marco van Basten, Ruud Gullit and Frank Rijkaard, got no further than the last 16 where they were beaten 2-1 by old enemies Germany.

• Four years later the Netherlands were among the favourites to triumph at USA '94 but, once more, failed to live up to expectations. After knocking out Jack Charlton's Republic of Ireland side, the Dutch went out in the quarter-finals to the eventual winners Brazil, losing an entertaining game 3-2.

• At the 1998 finals in France, though, the Netherlands did considerably better, making it to the semi-finals before losing to Brazil again – this time on penalties. Disappointed by this defeat, they lost the third place match to surprise package Croatia, but it was still their best showing since the near glory days of the Seventies.

• The Netherlands first appeared at the finals in 1934 in Italy but bowed out in the first round, losing 3-2 to Switzerland. It was a similar story four years later when the Dutch went out 3-0 to Czechoslovakia.

• The Netherlands had to wait until 1974 before they reached the finals again, but they certainly made up for lost time. Orchestrated and captained by the brilliant Johan Cruyff and playing a free-flowing game dubbed 'Total Football', the Dutch reached the final where they faced hosts West Germany in Munich. In the first minute Cruyff won a penalty which Johan Neeskens converted, but the

Germans fought back to win 2-1.

• Fours years later the Dutch stormed through two group stages to reach the final for a second time, where their opponents were once again the hosts, Argentina. On this occasion the Netherlands managed to take the game to extra-time, but they eventually succumbed 3-1. Despite their lack of silverware, however, the Netherlands' attacking style of play won them many admirers around the world and the general consensus is that they were the best international team of the Seventies.

• The Dutch had to wait until 1990 before returning to the finals but, despite fielding

• The Netherlands surprisingly missed out on the 2002 World Cup in Japan and Korea, but they were back for the 2006 finals in Germany. Yet again, though, they failed to live up to the pre-tournament hype, bowing out in the last 16 to Portugal after breezing through a so-called 'Group of Death'.

PREVIOUS TOURNAMENTS

1930 Did not enter	1962 Did not qualify	1986 Did not qualify
1934 Round 1	1966 Did not qualify	1990 Round 2
1938 Round 1	1970 Did not qualify	1994 Quarter-finals
1950 Did not enter	1974 Runners-up	1998 Fourth place
1954 Did not enter	1978 Runners-up	2002 Did not qualify
1958 Did not qualify	1982 Did not qualify	2006 Round 2

DENMARK

Denmark will boast one of the most experienced line-ups at the finals, a number of their key players being veterans of their last campaign in 2002 when the Danes reached the last 16 before losing to England. It would be easy to assume, then, that Morten Olsen's side might now be over-the-hill but any country that under-estimates Denmark will do so at their peril.

Proof that the Danes should not be dismissed as a 'Dad's Army' XI came in the qualifiers when they topped a difficult group including Portugal, Hungary and ancient rivals Sweden. Denmark's performance in Lisbon, when they overturned Portugal's 2-1 lead to win with two goals in the last two minutes, was arguably the most stunning victory by any team in the qualifying round.

> **"I like to play with quick, wide players because they can cause the opponent particular problems."**
>
> Denmark coach
> Morten Olsen

The Danes' first-choice team contains many familiar names to Premiership fans, including Stoke City goalkeeper Thomas Sorensen, Liverpool defender Daniel Agger, former Charlton winger Dennis Rommedahl and Arsenal striker Nicklas Bendtner. The team are usually sent out in an attacking 4-3-3 formation by Olsen, with Rommedahl and another experienced campaigner, Fiorentina's Martin Jorgensen, providing the ammunition for Bendtner from the flanks. With the two (unrelated) Poulsens, Jakob and Christian, rarely straying from central midfield, the most likely source of goals from this area comes from the 33-year-old Jon Dahl Tomasson, who has figured on the scoresheet more than 50 times for his country.

Like many of his players, Denmark's coach is no stranger to the international scene. The first ever Dane to win 100 caps, Olsen has been in charge of the national team since 2000 but is said to be keen to return to club football after the finals. He and his senior players will be keen to sign off in style, but Denmark might fall just short in a tough group.

DENMARK AT THE WORLD CUP

• An exciting Danish side featuring the attacking talents of Michael Laudrup, Preben Elkjaer and Jesper Olsen breezed through the group stages at their first World Cup in 1986, beating Scotland (1-0), Uruguay (6-1) and West Germany (2-0). However, the Danes came unstuck against Spain in the first knock-out round, losing 5-1 despite taking the lead.

• **The Danes went one better at their next World Cup in 1998, reaching the quarter-finals after demolishing Nigeria 4-1 in the last 16 with the two Laudrups, Michael and younger brother Brian, to the fore. Denmark played brilliantly in their next match against Brazil, but went home after narrowly losing out in a five-goal thriller.**

• Denmark got through the group stages again at the 2002 finals, their most notable victory coming against reigning world champions France. In the last 16, though, they were easily beaten by England, with Rio Ferdinand, Michael Owen and, no doubt to the surprise of his team-mates, Emile Heskey all finding the net in a convincing 3-0 win for Sven Goran Eriksson's team.

PREVIOUS TOURNAMENTS

1930 Did not enter	1962 Did not enter	1986 Round 2
1934 Did not enter	1966 Did not qualify	1990 Did not qualify
1938 Did not enter	1970 Did not qualify	1994 Did not qualify
1950 Did not enter	1974 Did not qualify	1998 Quarter-finals
1954 Did not enter	1978 Did not qualify	2002 Round 2
1958 Did not qualify	1982 Did not qualify	2006 Did not qualify

KEY PLAYER:
CHRISTIAN POULSEN

Danish Player of the Year in both 2005 and 2006, headband-wearing midfielder Christian Poulsen has won over 70 caps for Denmark since making his international debut in 2001.

Previously with Copenhagen, Schalke and Sevilla, the 30-year-old currently plays for Juventus but has struggled to hold down a regular place with the Serie A giants. However, his performances for his country have not suffered as a result, and his typically industrious displays were a feature of the Danes' impressive qualifying campaign. A tough tackler whose ball-winning skills provide a platform for his team's three-pronged attack, Poulsen has had his fair share of disciplinary problems and was suspended when Denmark limped out of the 2002 World Cup against England. He was badly missed that day, and will be again if he falls foul of the officials in South Africa.

JAPAN

Japan have made remarkable progress since the J-League, the country's first professional football league, was set up in 1992. The Blue Samarai, as they are known to their fans, have qualified for the previous three World Cups and will go to South Africa with hopes of matching their performance as hosts in 2002 when they progressed to the second round.

Managed by Takeshi Okada, who also coached his country at France '98, Japan qualified for the finals with some ease although they were eventually pipped for first place in their group by Australia. Since booking their passage, however, they have suffered a major setback when first-choice goalkeeper Yoshikatsu Kawaguchi broke his leg in a club match. If he does not recover in time to play at a fourth World Cup, his most likely deputy is another experienced keeper, Seigo Narazaki of Nagoya Grampus.

Japan's back four is also made up of locally-based players, and they will require support from a midfield which is where the team's true quality lies. Former Celtic star Shunsuke Nakamura is the central figure but he will be ably assisted by Wolfsburg's Makoto Hasebe, who in 2009 became only the second Japanese player to win the Bundesliga title, and by the terrier-like Junichi Imamoto, now with Rennes after five years in English football with Arsenal, Fulham, West Brom and Cardiff.

Okada normally favours a 4-2-3-1 system, which only leaves room for a single out-and-out striker. He may opt for the veteran Keiji Tamada of Nagoya Grampus or an exciting new talent, Shinji Okazaki, who in 2009 scored hat-tricks in consecutive matches against Hong Kong and Togo.

Drawn in a tough group, Japan will certainly be energetic and competitive, but the worry must be that they will eventually be over-powered by more muscular opponents.

> **"It will be a fourth World Cup finals for Japan and we are aiming for a top-four spot."**
>
> Japan coach Takeshi Okada

JAPAN AT THE WORLD CUP

• Japan first featured at the World Cup in 1998 but it proved to be a debut to forget as they crashed to three defeats against Argentina, Croatia and Jamaica. Japan's only goal was scored by striker Masashi Nakayama who, two years later, recorded the fastest ever hat-trick in international football when he struck three times inside the opening four minutes against Brunei.

• Japan fared better in 2002 when, as co-hosts with South Korea, they reached the first knock-out round after defeating both Russia (1-0) and Tunisia (2-0) in the group stage. The home fans, though, were soon crying into their sake when Turkey beat them 1-0 in the last 16.

• Japan made it to three finals on the trot in 2006, but performed poorly in Germany. After a disappointing 3-1 defeat by Australia they picked up a creditable point from a 0-0 draw with Croatia, but were then hammered 4-1 by Brazil to finish bottom of their group.

• Japan were the first team to qualify for the 2010 finals, clinching their place with a 1-0 win against Uzbekistan in Tashkent.

PREVIOUS TOURNAMENTS

1930 Did not enter	1962 Did not qualify	1986 Did not qualify
1934 Did not enter	1966 Did not enter	1990 Did not qualify
1938 Withdrew	1970 Did not qualify	1994 Did not qualify
1950 Banned	1974 Did not qualify	1998 Round 1
1954 Did not qualify	1978 Did not qualify	2002 Round 2
1958 Did not enter	1982 Did not qualify	2006 Round 1

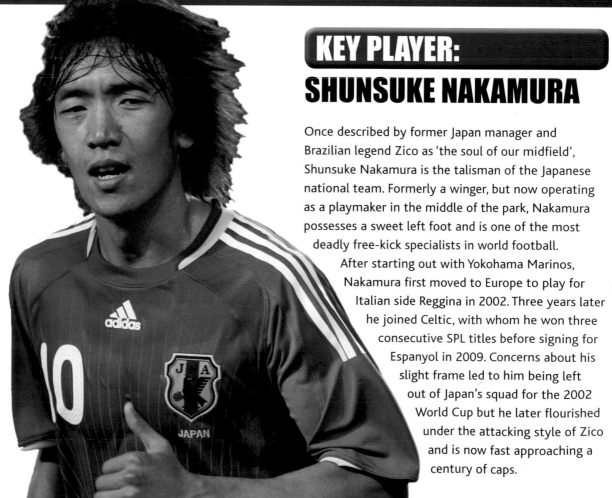

KEY PLAYER:
SHUNSUKE NAKAMURA

Once described by former Japan manager and Brazilian legend Zico as 'the soul of our midfield', Shunsuke Nakamura is the talisman of the Japanese national team. Formerly a winger, but now operating as a playmaker in the middle of the park, Nakamura possesses a sweet left foot and is one of the most deadly free-kick specialists in world football. After starting out with Yokohama Marinos, Nakamura first moved to Europe to play for Italian side Reggina in 2002. Three years later he joined Celtic, with whom he won three consecutive SPL titles before signing for Espanyol in 2009. Concerns about his slight frame led to him being left out of Japan's squad for the 2002 World Cup but he later flourished under the attacking style of Zico and is now fast approaching a century of caps.

CAMEROON

Cameroon are old stagers at the World Cup and in South Africa will make their sixth appearance at the finals – a record unmatched by any other African side. Although the Indomitable Lions have only once made it beyond the group stages they always provide strong opposition and it will be no different this time around.

For a while, though, it appeared highly unlikely that Cameroon would figure at the finals at all. After picking up just one point from their first two fixtures in the qualifiers, their World Cup dream seemed to be over. It was revived, however, when former Rangers manager Paul Le Guen replaced Otto Pfister at the helm. The change at the top transformed the Lions' form, and they eventually booked their place in South Africa with a 2-0 win in Morocco.

"The key has been the talent of the players," Le Guen modestly said after this victory. Whatever his own personal contribution, the Frenchman was surely correct to point to the ability in the squad, because Cameroon possess some outstanding performers. Chief among them is brilliant Inter Milan striker Samuel Eto'o, a two-time Champions League winner with his previous club, Barcelona. At the other end of the pitch, the Lions' defence boasts the Tottenham duo Sebastien Bassong and Benoit Assou-Ekotto, while alongside Arsenal's Alex Song in midfield there may be room for two veterans: Newcastle's Geremi and Rigobert Song, once of Liverpool. The goalkeeper will almost certainly be Carlos Kameni of Espanyol, an excellent shot-stopper who is known to Cameroon fans as 'The Phenomenon'.

The Lions have landed in a tricky group but they are a strong, powerful side and will fancy their chances of reaching the second round at the very least.

> **"The way we finished our qualifying campaign has given us real confidence. I'm certain we can get second place in the group."**
>
> Cameroon coach Paul Le Guen

CAMEROON AT THE WORLD CUP

• Cameroon performed well at their first World Cup in 1982, drawing all three of their group games (including a spirited 1-1 draw with eventual winners Italy) and only missed out on a second-round place on goals scored.

• The African side did even better at their next finals in 1990, sensationally beating reigning champions Argentina 1-0 in their opening match despite having two players sent off. Inspired by veteran striker Roger Milla, Cameroon went on to reach the quarter-finals where they lost a pulsating tie 3-2 to England.

• Milla became the oldest player ever to appear at the finals, when he pulled on the green Cameroon shirt again at the 1994 tournament in the USA at the age of 42. In his side's final match he scored a consolation goal in a 6-1 defeat by Russia to become the oldest player ever to score at the World Cup.

• At their last finals in 2002 Cameroon planned to wear sleeveless shirts until FIFA ruled against them, on the basis that the tops were 'vests' rather than proper shirts.

PREVIOUS TOURNAMENTS

1930 Did not enter	1962 Did not enter	1986 Did not qualify
1934 Did not enter	1966 Withdrew	1990 Quarter-finals
1938 Did not enter	1970 Did not qualify	1994 Round 1
1950 Did not enter	1974 Did not qualify	1998 Round 1
1954 Did not enter	1978 Did not qualify	2002 Round 1
1958 Did not enter	1982 Round 1	2006 Did not qualify

KEY PLAYER:
ALEX SONG

The nephew of Cameroon legend Rigobert Song, Alex Song has emerged as a vital player for his country in the last 18 months after making his international debut against Egypt in the 2008 African Nations Cup. Following a number of eye-catching performances, Song was voted into the team of the tournament, and he hasn't looked back since. A versatile player who can perform either in defence or the centre of midfield, Song's chief assets are his strength, athleticism and tackling ability, but he also passes the ball well and can shoot with power from distance.

Song, 22, started out with French club Bastia before moving to Arsenal for £1 million in 2006.

After a loan spell at Charlton he eventually established himself in the Gunners side in the 2008/09 campaign and has become an automatic selection in Arsene Wenger's line-up.

ITALY

Reigning champions Italy travel to South Africa with hopes of winning the World Cup for a fifth time, equalling Brazil's record. However, they will be aware that history is against them, as no team has managed to retain the trophy since the South Americans' consecutive triumphs in 1958 and 1962. Still, the Italians are a vastly experienced side and will be serious contenders.

Italy qualified fairly comfortably for the finals, winning their group ahead of Ireland after a 2-2 draw in Dublin. To the delight of their fans, the Azzurri then got lucky at the World Cup draw, landing an apparently easy group with Paraguay, Slovakia and New Zealand.

As ever, the Italians will be strong at the back. Goalkeeper Gianluigi Buffon is arguably the best in the world in his position, while his Juventus team-mates Fabio Cannavaro and Giorgi Chiellini are a formidable pairing in central defence. The midfield, too, has impressive performers in Milan's Andrea Pirlo, Roma's Daniele

> **"Every opponent is formidable if we give a little look towards the last 16 and quarter-finals."**
> Italy coach Marcello Lippi

de Rossi and Juve's Mauro Camoranesi, but further forward, Italy have problems. With the brilliant but inconsistent Francisco Totti currently in self-imposed international retirement, the team lacks a world-class striker. Juve's Vincenzo Iaquinta and Fiorentina's Alberto Gilardino are the most likely starters, but rising star Giuseppe Rossi could also get an opportunity at some point. The Villarreal striker has an impressive goalscoring record at club level, and would add a touch of youthful zest to one of the oldest teams at the finals.

Lippi will ensure that Italy are well-organised and difficult to beat, and they should top their undemanding group with something to spare. Once the knock-out stages begin, however, they may struggle to score goals and a lack of pace among some of their numerous veterans could also be exposed.

THE GAFFER: MARCELLO LIPPI

Marcello Lippi is in his second spell at the helm of the Azzurri, the first having ended gloriously when Italy won the 2006 World Cup. Three days after that triumph Lippi decided not to renew his contract, and was replaced by Roberto Donadoni. However, Donadoni was sacked after Italy's uninspiring Euro 2008 campaign, and the Italian FA turned once again to Lippi.

A central defender in his playing days with Sampdoria, Lippi began his coaching career with a variety of lower division clubs. His big break came when he joined Napoli, who he led to the UEFA Cup in 1994. That same year Lippi moved to Juventus, where he won the Champions League in 1996 and three Serie A titles before joining Inter Milan in 1999. After one unsuccessful season at the San Siro, he returned to Juve and collected another two Serie A titles prior to becoming Italy's coach for the first time in 2004.

Now 61, the silver-haired Lippi has a reputation for being tactically flexible. "I don't like coaches who force players to fit in with their system," he said recently. "Football, like life itself, isn't perfect, and that's the way I like it."

KEY PLAYER: ANDREA PIRLO

A midfield playmaker who can either play in front of the back four or just behind the strikers, Andrea Pirlo's importance to the Italian side is summed up by the nickname given to him by his international team-mates – l'architetto ('The Architect').

Now aged 30, Pirlo started out with Brescia before moving to Inter Milan in 1998. However, his career only really took off when, three years later, he swapped dressing rooms at the San Siro and joined city rivals AC Milan for around £14 million. Given a deeper midfield role by manager Carlo Ancelotti, Pirlo thrived in a Milan side that went on to enjoy huge success, winning one Scudetto and two Champions League titles in 2003 and 2007.

A superb passer of the ball over a variety of distances, Pirlo won his first cap for Italy in 2002. Four years later he starred for his country at the World Cup in Germany, receiving the Man of the Match award for his performance against France in the final in Berlin.

ONE TO WATCH: GIUSEPPE ROSSI

Born in New Jersey in 1987, Giuseppe Rossi turned down the chance to play for the USA at the last World Cup because his dream was always to wear the blue of Italy, the original home of his immigrant parents. The young striker realised that ambition in 2008 when he came on as a sub against Bulgaria, but only after his football career had taken him to three different countries.

Rossi left the States as a teenager to join Parma's youth academy, but his potential was soon spotted by bigger European clubs. In 2005 he was snapped up by Manchester United, where Sir Alex Ferguson hailed him as the club's best finisher since Paul Scholes. Rossi, though, only scored one goal for United before being shipped out on loan, first to Newcastle and then back to Parma. In 2007 he was sold to Villarreal for £6.7 million, and it was in Spain that Rossi finally established himself, averaging a goal every other game over the next two seasons.

A deadly poacher inside the box, he could be a surprise star of the finals in South Africa.

TACTICS BOARD: PIRLO THE PEARL

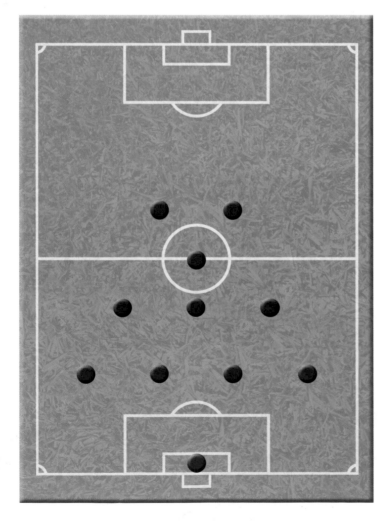

The most important player in the Italy team is Andrea Pirlo; if the Milan star performs well, then so do the Azzurri. For years Pirlo was Italy's deep-lying playmaker, but recently coach Marcello Lippi has devised a new role for him as a creator tucked in behind two strikers.

If Lippi continues with this experiment then Italy will line up in South Africa in a 4-3-1-2 formation, with Pirlo providing the ammunition for Alberto Gilardino and either Vincenzo Iaquinta or Giuseppe Rossi. Behind him, a midfield trio, including Daniele de Rossi and Mauro Camoranesi, will do the donkey work, closing down the opposition quickly, winning tackles and seeking to get Pirlo on the ball as often as possible.

For the plan to work, though, Pirlo must find space and he may find that difficult if he is tracked by a man-marker.

ITALY AT THE WORLD CUP

• Italy won the World Cup at the first attempt as hosts in 1934, beating Czechoslovakia 2-1 in the final in Rome. Their first goal was scored by left-winger Raimondo Orsi, with a freakishly swerving right foot shot. The following day he tried to repeat the shot 20 times for the benefit of photographers – but, even without a goalkeeper, he failed to hit the target.

• **Italy retained the trophy in 1938 after beating Yugoslavia 4-2 in the final in Paris. With World War II postponing the next tournament until 1950 Italy could claim to be world champions for a record total of 16 years.**

• At the 1966 World Cup in England, Italy were surprisingly eliminated at the group stage after losing 1-0 to minnows North Korea – one of the biggest shocks in the history of the tournament. When the Italian squad arrived back at Genoa Airport they were pelted with rotten tomatoes by hundreds of angry fans.

• **The Italians had to wait until 1970 before reaching the final again, but were crushed 4-1 by a brilliant Brazil team. Italy, though, could look back on their tournament with pride, especially a thrilling 4-3 win against West Germany in the semi-final.**

Italy celebrate their fourth World Cup triumph four years ago

• In Spain in 1982 Italy won the World Cup for a third time, equalling a record set by Brazil, after a 3-1 defeat of West Germany in the final in Madrid. The Italians, however, had made hard work of the group stage, sneaking through with three draws against Cameroon, Peru and Poland.

• **In 1990 Italy hosted the finals for a second time but had to be satisfied with third place after losing on penalties to Argentina in the semi-finals. There was some consolation, though, for bug-eyed Italian striker Toto Schillaci, whose six goals in the** tournament won him the Golden Boot.

• At USA '94 Italy became the first team to lose a World Cup final in a penalty shoot-out. Three Italians missed from the spot, including pony-tailed striker Roberto Baggio who blazed his kick high over the bar to gift the trophy to Brazil.

• **The Italians had better luck in 2006, winning the final on penalties against France after a 1-1 draw in the Olympic Stadium, Berlin. Defender Fabio Grosso scored the winning penalty to give the Italians a 5-3 victory in the shoot-out.**

PREVIOUS TOURNAMENTS

1930 Did not enter	1962 Round 1	1986 Round 2
1934 Winners	1966 Round 1	1990 Third place
1938 Winners	1970 Runners-up	1994 Runners-up
1950 Round 1	1974 Round 1	1998 Quarter-finals
1954 Round 1	1978 Fourth place	2002 Round 2
1958 Did not qualify	1982 Winners	2006 Winners

PARAGUAY

Appearing at their fourth-straight World Cup, Paraguay will hope to continue the good form they showed in the qualifying round when they beat both Brazil and Argentina on their way to finishing third in the South American group. Their fans, meanwhile, will take great heart from a kind draw which seems to open a clear path to the knock-out stages.

Under Argentinean coach Gerardo Martino, Paraguay have evolved into a solid, counter-attacking team built on a mean defence. They conceded just 16 goals in 18 qualifiers, a record only bettered by Brazil amongst their South American rivals, and in exactly half their matches they managed to keep a clean sheet. Experienced goalkeeper and skipper Justo Villar, who plays his club football in Spain with Valladolid, performed superbly throughout the campaign and he was ably assisted by Boca Juniors' Julio Caceres and Sunderland's Paulo da Silva in central defence.

> **"A good result against Italy in the first game is the most important for us."**
>
> Paraguay coach
> Gerardo Martino

Paraguay generally play an orthodox 4-4-2 system, although Martino sometimes switches to 4-3-3. Either way, the main source of creativity is Christian Riveros, a talented passer of the ball who plays in Mexico for Cruz Azul. Up front, Manchester City's Roque Santa Cruz is the main man, although he can rely on good support from free-kick specialist Oscar Cardozo, a prolific scorer with Benfica in recent seasons. Another striking option is provided by Borussia Dortmund's Haedo Valdez who, like Santa Cruz, is particularly strong in the air.

On their previous seven appearances at the finals Paraguay have never been able to overcome the second round hurdle, falling at this stage on three occasions. This time around they again have every chance of progressing from their group, but the Albirroja will do extremely well to survive a likely last 16 meeting with Holland.

PARAGUAY AT THE WORLD CUP

• Paraguay's three games at the 1958 finals in Sweden produced an incredible total of 21 goals – a record for the group stage. The South Americans' first match was an extraordinary 7-3 defeat by France, and they followed that up with a 3-2 win over Scotland and a 3-3 draw with Yugoslavia.

• In 1986 Paraguay boss Cayetano Re became the first coach to be dismissed during the finals. His crime was to stand too close to the pitch during his team's 2-2 draw with Belgium, a result that put Paraguay into the second round of the tournament for the first time.

• Paraguay were the first team to be knocked out of the World Cup on the 'Golden Goal' rule which applied at the 1998 and 2002 tournaments.

Facing hosts France in the second round in 1998 the South Americans were eliminated by Laurent Blanc's 114th minute goal which, under the terms of the rule, ended the match.

• Paraguay's goalkeeper at the 1998 and 2002 tournaments was the eccentric Jose Luis Chilavert, who scored a world record eight goals during his international career.

PREVIOUS TOURNAMENTS

1930 Round 1	1962 Did not qualify	1986 Round 2
1934 Did not enter	1966 Did not qualify	1990 Did not qualify
1938 Did not enter	1970 Did not qualify	1994 Did not qualify
1950 Round 1	1974 Did not qualify	1998 Round 2
1954 Did not qualify	1978 Did not qualify	2002 Round 2
1958 Round 1	1982 Did not qualify	2006 Round 1

KEY PLAYER:
ROQUE SANTA CRUZ

The second highest ever scorer for Paraguay, Roque Santa Cruz made his international debut at the tender age of 17, soon after impressing in the 1999 World Youth Cup. An excellent all-round striker who excels in the air, Santa Cruz will be appearing at his third World Cup this summer, having also figured in his country's campaigns in 2002 and 2006.

At club level, Santa Cruz spent eight years with Bayern Munich, helping the German giants win three Bundesliga titles and the Champions League in 2001, before signing for Blackburn in 2007. Two years later he followed his former boss at Ewood Park, Mark Hughes, to moneybags Manchester City in a £17.5 million deal. However, he has so far struggled to make an impact in a City side in which competition for attacking places is exceptionally fierce.

NEW ZEALAND

Appearing at only their second ever World Cup, New Zealand have done superbly simply to reach the finals in South Africa. Hailing from a country where football trails some way behind rugby and cricket in popularity, the All Whites will be especially keen to make a big impression this summer but their lack of quality could be exposed by their group opponents.

Even if, as many expect, New Zealand return home empty-handed they will enjoy their experience of playing on the world stage for the first time since 1982. They booked their passage this time around thanks to a hard-fought play-off victory against Bahrain, a single goal by Plymouth striker Rory Fallon deciding the tie, although a penalty save from goalkeeper Mark Paston was equally vital to their eventual success. The All Whites' achievement in qualifying was all the more remarkable when you consider that there is only one professional club in New Zealand, Wellington Phoenix, and even they compete hundreds of miles away from home in the Australian A-League.

In a squad not exactly bursting with well-known names Blackburn's Ryan Nelsen and Celtic striker Chris Killen have a higher profile than most, while defender Ivan Vicelich, his country's highest-capped player, spent a long time in Holland with Roda JC and RKC Waalwijk. Otherwise, the Kiwis' side is largely made up of journeymen such as striker Shane Smeltz, formerly of AFC Wimbledon and now plying his trade back 'Down Under' with Gold Coast United.

Technically limited, the All Whites will have to rely on organizational skills to make themselves competitive. They will be helped by having a coach, Ricki Herbert, who is not afraid to improvise but, even so, it will be a surprise if they avoid defeat in any of their games.

> **"We'll be going there with very strong ambitions to make a statement and make it as difficult as we can."**
>
> New Zealand coach
> Ricki Herbert

NEW ZEALAND AT THE WORLD CUP

• In qualifying for their only previous finals, in Spain in 1982, New Zealand set numerous records. They travelled more miles (55,000), played more games (15) and scored more goals (44) than any team to qualify before then. In addition, their 13-0 annihilation of Fiji in Auckland was the biggest victory in World Cup history at the time.

• **Predictably, the All Whites found it far tougher at the finals. However, in their first match against Scotland in Malaga they gave Jock Stein's side a scare by scoring twice after going 3-0 down in the first half. The Scots, though, added two late goals through John Robertson and Steve Archibald to win 5-2.**

• In their second match New Zealand went down 3-0 to the Soviet Union, and with their final fixture being against the brilliant Brazil side of Zico, Socrates and Falcao, even their most ardent of fans was not anticipating anything except a heavy defeat. Given the huge gulf in ability between the two teams, the All Whites' subsequent 4-0 loss was no disgrace.

PREVIOUS TOURNAMENTS

1930 Did not enter	1962 Did not enter	1986 Did not qualify
1934 Did not enter	1966 Did not enter	1990 Did not qualify
1938 Did not enter	1970 Did not qualify	1994 Did not qualify
1950 Did not enter	1974 Did not qualify	1998 Did not qualify
1954 Did not enter	1978 Did not qualify	2002 Did not qualify
1958 Did not enter	1982 Round 1	2006 Did not qualify

KEY PLAYER:
RYAN NELSEN

A solid defender who never shies away from a physical challenge and poses a major attacking threat at set-pieces, Ryan Nelsen is both New Zealand's captain and the team's outstanding player. First capped by his country in 1999 against Poland, a succession

of injuries prevented him from making a single appearance for the Kiwis between 2004-08, but it is no surprise that his return to the side has seen a revival in their fortunes.

Nelsen began his club career with DC United in the USA after having gained a degree in political science from Stanford University. His impressive performances earned him a move to Blackburn Rovers in 2005, since when he has established himself as a key member of the Premiership side's notoriously rugged defence.

SLOVAKIA

Slovakia are appearing at their first World Cup as an independent nation, having previously featured at the finals as half of Czechoslovakia. A kind draw has given them realistic hopes of reaching the knock-out stages, although much will depend on the outcome of their match with Paraguay who will also be battling for the second spot behind group favourites Italy.

Slovakia impressed in qualifying, topping a tough group that also included Slovenia, Poland, Northern Ireland and arch rivals the Czech Republic. The key result for the Slovaks was a 2-1 victory against their neighbours in Prague, a victory that has already attained legendary status back in their homeland. However, it was another good away way win - against the Poles in Chorzow – that ultimately clinched their place in South Africa.

> "I think that there are harder groups than ours, but facing Italy is always fascinating."
>
> Slovakia captain
> Marek Hamsik

Coached by Vladimir Weiss, a former Czechoslovak international who helped his country reach the quarter-finals at Italia '90, Slovakia are a competitive, battling side short of star names. An exception is captain Marek Hamsik, a skilful midfielder with a goalscorer's instinct, who plays for Italian side Napoli. Other well-known players include Liverpool stopper Martin Skrtel and diminutive Chelsea winger Miroslav Stoch, who has earned rave reviews during a loan spell with Steve McClaren's FC Twente. Elsewhere, the Slovaks appear to be short of genuine quality, although Legia Warsaw goalkeeper Jan Mucha is a more than capable performer and experienced striker Robert Vittek has a reasonable strike rate at international level. The squad should also include the coach's son, Vladimir Weiss jnr, despite his failure to make much of an impression at Manchester City.

Slovakia will not be a pushover but a 4-0 friendly defeat by England in 2009 suggests they will struggle against top opposition if they make it out of the group stage.

SLOVAKIA AT THE WORLD CUP

• Competing as the 'Slovakia' part of Czechoslovakia, the team reached the World Cup final at their first attempt in 1934. Facing hosts Italy in Rome, Czechoslovakia took the lead with 20 minutes remaining through Antonin Puc, but the Italians quickly equalized and went on to score a winner in extra-time.

• In 1962 Czechoslovakia made it to the final again, this time facing Brazil in the Chilean capital Santiago. Once again, the Czechs took the lead, European Footballer of the Year Josef Masopust striking early in the first half. Brazil, though, were not to be denied and eventually won 3-1.

• Czechoslovakia met England twice at the World Cup. In 1970 a penalty by Leeds striker Allan Clarke gave England the points, and the countries were drawn in the same group again in 1982. This time England won 2-0, thanks to strikes by Trevor Francis and an unwitting Czech defender.

• In their last ever World Cup in Italy in 1990, Czechoslovakia reached the quarter-finals before going down 1-0 to eventual winners Germany.

PREVIOUS TOURNAMENTS

1930 Did not enter	1962 Runners-up	1986 Did not qualify
1934 Runners-up	1966 Did not qualify	1990 Quarter-finals
1938 Quarter-finals	1970 Round 1	1994 Did not qualify
1950 Did not enter	1974 Did not qualify	1998 Did not qualify
1954 Round 1	1978 Did not qualify	2002 Did not qualify
1958 Round 1	1982 Round 1	2006 Did not qualify

* Competed as Czechoslovakia (1930-94)

KEY PLAYER:
MAREK HAMSIK

An attacking, technically gifted midfielder who has been compared to Frank Lampard, Slovakia captain Marek Hamsik is his country's main creative force. Aged just 22, Hamsik made his international debut in 2007 and starred in Slovakia's World Cup qualifying campaign.

Starting out with Slovan Bratislava, Hamsik moved to Italian side Brescia when he was only 22. In 2007 he joined Napoli for around £4 million, and went on to be top scorer for the Serie A outfit in the next two seasons. A good World Cup could see Hamsik move to the Premiership, with Chelsea among those clubs said to be interested in signing him.

"I think he's crucial to our chances in South Africa," says Slovakia coach Vladimir Weiss. "He has an attitude I like, he's very single minded."

BRAZIL

The only country to have appeared at all the previous finals, five-time winners Brazil are always among the favourites to lift the trophy. That is very much the case this year, too, with the 'Little Canary', as they are affectionately known, leading the South American challenge. A team full of star names, including midfield maestro Kaka, Brazil will certainly take some stopping.

Brazil topped their qualifying group, clinching their place in the finals with a hugely satisfying 3-1 win away to old enemies Argentina. Their campaign, though, also featured no fewer than four 0-0 home draws to the frustration of their huge army of passionate fans. Indeed, after consecutive stalemates against no-hopers Bolivia and Colombia, and with Brazil's qualification hopes hanging in the balance, the home crowd chanted for the head of the team's coach, former World Cup-winning captain Dunga.

The embattled Dunga eventually came through that crisis, but criticism remains of his tactics, which are perceived by many in Brazil as overly negative. The purists would love to see a return to the samba style of the past, but they won't get it under Dunga, whose approach values solidity and efficiency above flair and flamboyance. As a result, there is no room in Dunga's team for step-over king Ronaldinho, although the coach has said the AC Milan star could return if he ups his work-rate.

With or without Ronaldinho, Brazil will be hard to beat. They have a good goalkeeper in Inter Milan's Julio Cesar, a strong defence marshalled by his team-mate Lucio, creative midfielders in Kaka and Robinho, and a prolific goalscorer in Sevilla's Luis Fabiano. Robust, powerful and fast, Brazil don't concede many goals and are particularly dangerous at free-kicks, corners and on the counter-attack.

It will take a very good team indeed to knock them out.

> "Every time Brazil takes the field, we're expected to win. The pressure will be tough."
>
> Brazil coach Dunga

THE GAFFER: DUNGA

The captain of Brazil's World Cup-winning side of 1994, Dunga became his country's coach in 2006 despite having no prior experience at club level. A novice he may be, but Dunga has already won silverware, guiding Brazil to victory in the Copa America in 2007 and the Confederations Cup two years later.

A defensive midfielder in his playing days with clubs in Brazil, Italy, Germany and Japan, Dunga was a gritty, no-nonsense performer who gave the distinct impression that, even though he was briefly on the books of Rio outfit Vasco da Gama, he didn't spend any time juggling a ball in front of an audience of bikini-clad beauties on Copacabana beach.

Dunga has brought a similar pragmatism to the Brazilian side, angering critics who argue that his counter-attacking tactics are at odds with the country's traditionally attractive style, known locally as jogo bonito ('Play Beautiful'). The man in charge, though, is unrepentant. "Ever since we took over," Dunga said recently, "we've been trying to make our players, who are all stars with their club sides, become workers on the pitch."

Judging by Brazil's results, it's a message his players have taken to heart.

KEY PLAYER:
LUIS FABIANO

If Brazil are going to win the World Cup then they will need to score lots of goals, and Sevilla striker Luis Fabiano is the man to get them.

Fast, direct, strong in the air and possessing a powerful shot in both feet, Luis Fabiano has emerged from Ronaldo's shadow to become Brazil's undisputed leading frontman. Now aged 29, he has had a rollercoaster career with as many lows as highs, and for a while was known as 'the bad boy' of Brazilian football following a series of on-pitch brawls. Most notoriously, he once karate-kicked a River Plate player just below the neck before proudly announcing that he "would rather attack an Argentine than take a penalty". He has mellowed, though, since moving four years ago to Sevilla, where he has formed a prolific striking partnership with former West Ham and Tottenham star Freddie Kanoute.

A regular in the Brazil side since 2007, Luis Fabiano has an equally impressive goalscoring record at international level, most recently topping the scoring charts at the 2009 Confederations Cup with five goals.

ONE TO WATCH: ROBINHO

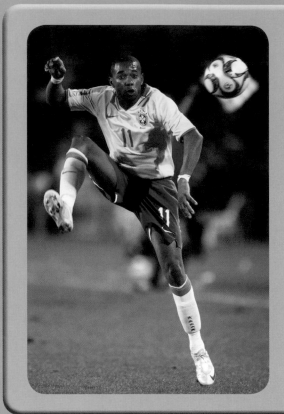

An enigmatic winger who can be dazzling one week and virtually anonymous the next, Robinho became the most expensive player in British football history when he joined Manchester City from Real Madrid for £32.5 million in August 2008. His superb close control and clever tricks have made him a fans' favourite at Eastlands, although he has so far found it difficult to shine away from home.

Robinho started out with legendary Brazilian club Santos, with whom he won the domestic championship in 2002 and 2004. He joined Real in 2005 and two years later helped the Spanish titans win the league on the last day of the season.

Now aged 26, Robinho made his international debut in a 1-0 defeat of Mexico in 2003. Four years later he was a key figure as Brazil won the Copa America, claiming the Golden Boot with a total of six goals in the competition. In 2009 he played in every game for Brazil at the Confederations Cup in South Africa, helping his country win the tournament following a 3-2 victory over the USA in the final.

TACTICS BOARD: KAKA CRUCIAL

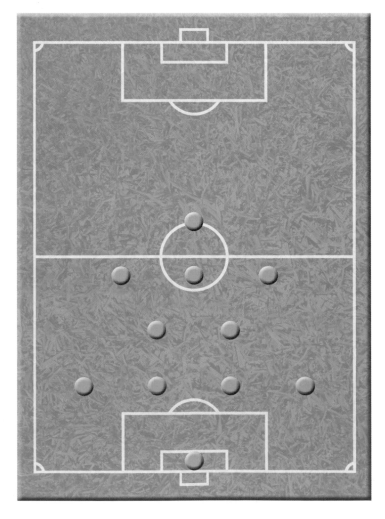

Brazil coach Dunga's favoured formation is a 4-2-3-1 system, in which two defensive midfielders fill the role played by the former World Cup-winning captain himself back in 1994. Former Arsenal skipper Gilberto Silva and Juventus scrapper Felipe Melo are the most likely players to occupy these positions, with the former also tasked with dropping into the back line when central defender Lucio makes one of his occasional charges forward.

The creative hub of the Brazilian side is Kaka, whose ability to pick out lone striker Luis Fabiano is crucial to the team's counter-attacking style. Alongside the AC Milan star, one-time Manchester City team-mates Robinho and Elano have the skills to undo the packed defences Brazil can expect to meet, while another attacking threat is posed by the surging runs of Inter Milan's Maicon from right-back. The left-back position has no regular occupant and this weak spot could be targeted by Brazil's opponents.

BRAZIL AT THE WORLD CUP

• Playing against Poland on a muddy pitch at the 1938 World Cup in France, Brazilian striker Leonidas da Silva threw away his boots and started to play barefoot. The referee made him put his boots back on, and Leonidas went on to score four goals as Brazil won a classic encounter 6-5.

• **As hosts in 1950 Brazil reached the final group of four teams and only needed to draw their last match against Uruguay to claim the trophy. However, despite taking the lead, Brazil lost the game 2-1 in front of nearly 200,000 disappointed fans in Rio.**

• Brazil won the World Cup for the first time in Sweden in 1958, beating the hosts 5-2 in the final in Stockholm. Two of their goals were scored by a brilliant 17-year-old called Pele, who became the youngest ever World Cup winner.

• **The South Americans retained their trophy in Chile four years later, beating Czechoslovakia 3-1 in the final in Santiago. Throughout the whole tournament Brazil only used 12 players.**

• With a magnificent side containing the likes of Pele, Rivelino and skipper Carlos Alberto, Brazil claimed an unprecedented third championship

Current Brazil manager Dunga (right) enjoys the celebrations in 1994

in Mexico in 1970 following a superb 4-1 demolition of Italy. Flying winger Jairzinho scored in every game at the finals, the last player to achieve this feat.

• **After 24 long years Brazil finally claimed a fourth trophy in 1994 in the USA. Again, Italy were their opponents in the final, although on this occasion Brazil only triumphed after a penalty shoot-out following a disappointing 0-0 draw.**

• Four years later Brazil reached the final again but a mystery illness to star striker Ronaldo in the build-up to kick-off disrupted their preparations, and they lost

3-0 to hosts France.

• **Brazil won the World Cup for a record fifth time in 2002 in Yokohama, Ronaldo scoring both goals in a 2-0 defeat of Germany in the final. Earlier, in the quarter-finals, Brazil had knocked England out thanks to a flukey free-kick by Ronaldinho which sailed over goalkeeper David Seaman's head.**

• The only country to appear at all 18 previous finals, Brazil crashed out of the 2006 tournament to France in the quarter-finals. There was some consolation, though, for Ronaldo who took his World Cup goals tally to 15, beating the old record of West German striker Gerd Muller.

PREVIOUS TOURNAMENTS

1930 Round 1	1962 Winners	1986 Quarter-finals
1934 Round 1	1966 Round 1	1990 Round 2
1938 Semi-finals	1970 Winners	1994 Winners
1950 Runners-up	1974 Fourth place	1998 Runners-up
1954 Quarter-finals	1978 Third place	2002 Winners
1958 Winners	1982 Round 2	2006 Quarter-finals

NORTH KOREA

At their only previous finals in 1966, North Korea famously caused a major upset by beating Italy on the way to the quarter-finals. The Asian minnows will hope to pull off a similar shock in South Africa but, realistically, their chances are extremely remote particularly as they have been drawn in the so-called 'Group of Death'.

Massive underdogs they may be, but the North Koreans have one great weapon at their disposal: the element of surprise. An unknown quantity outside Asia, they are a hard-working, defensively-minded side who play on the counter-attack. Although they don't score many goals, the Koreans don't concede many either and can make life difficult for opponents with a five-man backline that includes a sweeper.

North Korea's qualification campaign was not without controversy. After a 1-0 defeat away to bitter rivals South Korea their manager, Kim-Jong Hun, claimed that his players had been 'poisoned' by their hosts, an allegation that was dismissed as 'groundless and far-fetched' by South Korean officials. Despite that setback, the North Koreans made it to South Africa when they clinched second place in the group with a battling 0-0 draw in Saudi Arabia.

Their achievement in qualifying was all the more remarkable given that very few of their players have experience outside their own country. Among the exceptions are the team's captain, Hong Yong Jo, who plays in Russia for FC Rostov; Kawasaki Frontale striker Jong Tae-se, who has been dubbed 'the Asian Wayne Rooney' for his combative style; and holding midfielder An Young Hak, who plays his club football south of the border for Suwon Bluewings.

North Korea will certainly put up dogged resistance but, given the quality of the opposition they will face, the most likely scenario is that they will return pointless to Pyongyang.

> "There's no other team in the world who will be fighting with the same dedication to please the leader and bring fame to the motherland."
>
> North Korea coach Kim Jong Hun

NORTH KOREA AT THE WORLD CUP

• At their only previous finals in England in 1966 North Korea pulled off one of the biggest shocks in World Cup history when they beat Italy 1-0 at Ayresome Park, Middlesbrough. The win put the Red Mosquitoes, who were 1,000/1 outsiders at the start of the tournament, through to the quarter-finals while Italy were sensationally knocked out at the group stage.

• **North Korea's scorer on that famous afternoon was Pak Do Ik, a corporal in his country's army. In Italy he was dubbed 'the dentist' because his goal caused so much pain to a football-obsessed nation!**

• The Teeside public were captivated by the small, fast and skilful North Koreans and 3,000 local fans followed their adopted team to Liverpool for their quarter-final tie against Portugal at Goodison Park.

• **Amazingly, North Korea took a 3-0 lead against the mighty Portuguese, before the great Eusebio took charge to score four goals as the plucky underdogs were eventually beaten 5-3. The North Koreans' dream was over but their unlikely feats would be remembered for years to come.**

PREVIOUS TOURNAMENTS

1930 Did not enter	1962 Did not enter	1986 Did not qualify
1934 Did not enter	1966 Quarter-finals	1990 Did not qualify
1938 Did not enter	1970 Withdrew	1994 Did not qualify
1950 Did not enter	1974 Did not qualify	1998 Did not enter
1954 Did not enter	1978 Did not qualify	2002 Did not enter
1958 Did not enter	1982 Did not qualify	2006 Did not qualify

KEY PLAYER:
HONG YONG-JO

Very much the brain of the side, North Korea captain Hong Yong-Jo is a midfield playmaker who is invariably involved in his team's attacks. One of the few players to carry a goal threat in a largely defensive outfit, Hong also takes the majority of North Korea's set-pieces, including penalties. An outstanding performer in the qualifying round he also chipped in with three goals, notching two against Jordan and one against rivals South Korea.

One of a handful of North Koreans to play his club football outside the country, Hong initially left North Korean army side April 25 FC to play for Serbian club FK Bezanija in 2007. A year later he moved on to FC Rostov but has so far been unable to hold down a regular first-team place with the Russians.

IVORY COAST

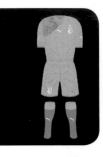

For some unknown reason, the football gods seem to have taken a dislike to the Ivory Coast. At their first World Cup in 2006 the Elephants were drawn in the so-called 'Group of Death' and exactly the same thing has happened this time around. However, the Ivorians are arguably the most talented team in Africa and will fancy their chances of taking points off all their group opponents.

One reason for their optimism, of course, is that in captain Didier Drogba the Elephants possess one of the best strikers in world football. An awesome sight when he is in full flow, Drogba is almost a one-man forward line but he has more than adequate support around him in the likes of Chelsea team-mate Salomon Kalou, Portsmouth hitman Aruna Dindane and Marseille striker Bakari Kune. Further back, Sevilla's Didier Zokora and Barcelona's Yaya Toure are powerful midfield performers while the latter's older brother, Manchester City's Kolo Toure, is the lynchpin of a defence that also includes Arsenal's Emmanuel Eboue. Where Ivory Coast might struggle, though, is in goal where a number of candidates have failed to make a decisive claim for the keeper's jersey. Boubacar Barry, who plays his club football in Belgium for Lokeren, is possibly the pick of a decidedly mixed bunch.

However, coach Vahid Halilhodzic, a former Yugoslav international who has managed a number of sides in France, won't be overly concerned by this apparent weakness as he knows his team are more than capable of taking the game to their World Cup opponents, even sides with the pedigree of group rivals Brazil and Portugal.

The Elephants' matches against this pair will be among the most eagerly anticipated of the first round stage. Whatever the outcomes of these mouthwatering encounters, fans around the globe can expect goals and entertainment galore.

> **"It's the toughest draw. Brazil and Portugal are the favourites but we will prepare to create an upset."**
> Ivory Coast coach Vahid Halilhodzic

IVORY COAST AT THE WORLD CUP

• Ivory Coast reached their first World Cup finals in 2006, but had the misfortune to be paired in the so-called 'Group of Death' with Argentina, Holland and Serbia & Montenegro.

• **Nonetheless, the Elephants performed reasonably well in Germany, providing Argentina with tough opposition in their first match before going down** to a 2-1 defeat. **Fittingly, star striker Didier Drogba, who had notched an impressive nine goals during the qualifying stages, grabbed Ivory Coast's consolation goal to go down in history as the first player from his country to score at the finals.**

• Another 2-1 defeat at the hands of Holland ended Ivory Coast's hopes of progressing to the second round, but they avoided the wooden spoon by fighting back from 2-0 down in their final match against Serbia & Montenegro to win 3-2. The Elephants' heroes were striker Aruna Dindane, who scored twice to level the scores, and substitute Bonaventure Kalou who slotted home the winner from the penalty spot with just four minutes left to play.

PREVIOUS TOURNAMENTS

1930 Did not enter	1962 Did not enter	1986 Did not qualify
1934 Did not enter	1966 Did not enter	1990 Did not qualify
1938 Did not enter	1970 Did not enter	1994 Did not qualify
1950 Did not enter	1974 Did not qualify	1998 Did not qualify
1954 Did not enter	1978 Did not qualify	2002 Did not qualify
1958 Did not enter	1982 Did not enter	2006 Round 1

KEY PLAYER:
KOLO TOURE

With the impressive attacking resources at their disposal Ivory Coast will score goals in South Africa, but will they be able to keep them out at the other end? Much will depend on the performances of Kolo Toure, the central pillar at the heart of the Elephants' back four.

With over 70 caps to his name already, the Manchester City defender is an experienced international campaigner and his pace, power and athleticism will be great assets to Ivory Coast, especially in their vital matches against group opponents against Brazil and Portugal.

Kolo Toure has come a long way since Arsenal snapped him up from Ivorian club ASEC Mimosas for a bargain £150,000 in 2002. A Premiership winner with the Gunners in 2004, he cost City £12 million when he moved to Eastlands five years later.

PORTUGAL

With 2008 World Footballer of the Year Cristiano Ronaldo in their ranks, Portugal will attract more attention than most sides in South Africa. But the Portuguese are far from a one-man team and, as they showed at the last World Cup when they finished fourth, they have the all-round quality to go a long way in the tournament.

What's more, the Portuguese will be desperate for a good showing at the finals after putting their fans through the wringer during their qualifying campaign. After a dismal start in which they picked up just six points from their opening five games, Portugal's chances of reaching South Africa appeared slim. However, to the relief of their under-fire coach Carlos Queiroz, they rallied sufficiently to finish second in their group behind Denmark before winning a play-off against Bosnia-Herzegovina.

Their qualifying difficulties behind them, Portugal have the ability to do well in South Africa despite being drawn in a nightmare group that also includes Brazil and the Ivory Coast. The team are solid at the back, where Chelsea's Ricardo Carvalho is an experienced presence. In midfield, Portugal have a good blend of steel and flair, while with Cristiano Ronaldo and Atletico Madrid's Simao flying down the wings their attack will take some stopping. Unsurprisingly, Queiroz has huge expectations of Ronaldo, saying, "I expect that in the World Cup he will win some games on his own."

While that may be true, it does rather suggest that Portugal may be over-reliant on their one true superstar. If they are to match or even better their achievements of 2006, Ronaldo will surely need to avoid injury or suspension. First, though, the Portuguese must fight their way out of 'The Group of Death' – and that won't be easy.

> **"I think we have a good chance. Of course, all the groups will be difficult for all the teams."**
> Portugal coach Carlos Queiroz

THE GAFFER: CARLOS QUEIROZ

Best known to Premiership fans as Sir Alex Ferguson's assistant at Manchester United, Carlos Queiroz replaced the Chelsea-bound Luiz Felipe Scolari as Portugal's coach in 2008. It was the second time Queiroz had held the position, having previously been in charge of the national team for two years during the early 1990s.

Born in Mozambique in 1953, Queiroz had a brief career as a player in the former Portuguese colony before building a reputation as a coach working with youth players. He led the Portuguese Under-20 team to two World Championships in 1989 and 1991 while developing the famous 'Golden Generation' of Portuguese players including Luis Figo, Rui Costa and goalkeeper Vitor Baia.

Later in the 1990s he managed Sporting Lisbon, New York MetroStars, Nagoya Grampus Eight and the United Arab Emirates before becoming South Africa coach in 2000. He guided the country to the 2002 World Cup but resigned before the finals after falling out with the South African FA.

In between two successful spells at Old Trafford, Queiroz spent a season a Ream Madrid but his failure to land either the La Liga title or the Champions League led to his dismissal after just 10 months

KEY PLAYER:
CRISTIANO RONALDO

Arguably the most exciting talent in world football today, Cristiano Ronaldo's brilliant dribbling skills and goalscoring ability will be crucial to Portugal's chances in South Africa.

Born on the Portuguese island of Madeira, Ronaldo began his career with Sporting Lisbon before joining Manchester United in a £12.25 million deal in 2003. In six years at Old Trafford he won a host of honours including the Champions League, the FA Cup and three Premiership titles. His most notable campaign was in 2007/08 when he scored an incredible 42 goals, a feat which helped him top the World Footballer of the Year poll in 2008. The following year he signed for Spanish giants Real Madrid for a world record £80 million.

Ronaldo made his international debut for Portugal against Kazakhstan in 2003 and the following year played for his country in their shock Euro 2004 final defeat by underdogs Greece. He first captained Portugal in 2007 and has since worn the skipper's armband on a regular basis.

ONE TO WATCH: JOAO MOUTINHO

One of the emerging talents in the Portuguese squad, 23-year-old Joao Moutinho is a versatile midfielder who can play in virtually any position across the middle of the pitch. Popular with supporters for his non-stop style of play, the Sporting Lisbon star is a tenacious and determined performer who passes the ball well and contributes the occasional goal.

Moutinho made his debut for Sporting in 2003 when he was just 17, wearing the number 28 shirt previously sported by a certain Cristiano Ronaldo. The following season he played every minute of the league campaign as Sporting finished second behind champions Porto. He was appointed the club's vice-captain when he was only 19, taking over the skipper's armband a year later to become Sporting's second youngest captain ever. Twice a winner of the Portuguese Cup with Sporting, in 2008 Moutinho was the subject of a failed £11.8 million bid from Everton.

He made his international debut in a friendly against Egypt in 2005 and has become a regular in the side in the last few years, appearing for the first time at a major tournament at Euro 2008.

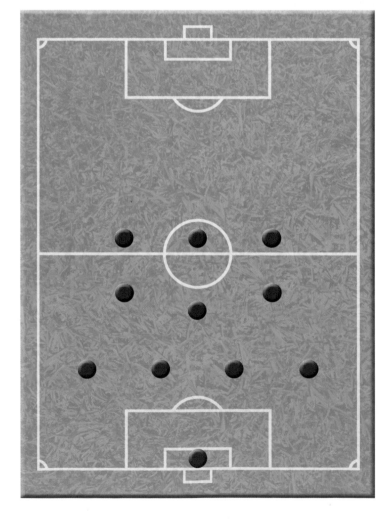

TACTICS BOARD:
FLYING WINGERS

A side who like to play on the counter-attack, Portugal will line up in South Africa in a 4-3-3 formation. Crucial to the system are the two wingers, Cristiano Ronaldo and Simao, who will support a lone central striker, most probably Sporting Lisbon's Liedson. Manchester United's Nani could also figure on the flanks, but is more likely to start on the bench.

In midfield, Real Madrid's Pepe has a largely defensive role, while alongside him Moutinho and Raul Meireles have more licence to get forward. Another option is the veteran Deco, an inventive attacking player who likes to play quick, short passes in and around the opposition penalty area.

The two full-backs, Chelsea's Jose Boswinga and Malaga's Duda, have important attacking roles as well as defensive ones while the two centre-backs, Ricardo Carvalho and Porto's Bruno Alves, are a strong pairing in front of goalkeeper Eduardo.

PORTUGAL AT THE WORLD CUP

• Portugal had to wait until 1966 before making their World Cup bow. They made up for lost time, though, by reaching the semi-finals where they lost 2-1 to hosts England at Wembley. In the previous round the Portuguese made one of the greatest comebacks ever at the finals, recovering from 3-0 down against North Korea to win 5-3.

• The brilliant Eusebio scored four of his country's goals in that match, and with nine goals in total was the tournament's leading scorer. Only three players – Juste Fontaine (13 goals for France in 1958), Sandor Kocsis (11 goals for Hungary in 1954) and Gerd Muller (10 goals for West Germany in 1970) – have found the net more often at a single World Cup.

• It was 20 years before Portugal reached the finals again, and they did so in style by clinching their place in Mexico with a 1-0 victory against West Germany in Stuttgart – the first time the Germans had been beaten at home in a competitive match.

• Portugal began the tournament superbly with a 1-0 victory over England, thanks to a goal by Carlos Manuel. However, a dispute about prize money disrupted the team's preparations for their remaining group games against **Poland and Morocco, and after two defeats the Portuguese were knocked out.**

• After another long wait, Portugal returned to the world stage for the 2002 finals. The so-called 'Golden Generation' was expected to perform well, but got off to an appalling start with a shock 3-2 defeat to the USA. A 4-0 thrashing of Poland seemed to put the Portuguese back on track, but in their final match their fate was sealed when they lost 1-0 to hosts South Korea.

• At the 2006 finals in Germany Portugal were involved in the dirtiest match in World Cup history, their last 16 encounter with Holland ending as a nine-a-side affair after two players from both teams were sent off. Russian referee Valentin Ivanov also waved the yellow card an unprecedented 16 times during Portugal's 1-0 win.

• In the quarter-finals Portugal beat England 3-1 on penalties after a 0-0 draw in Gelsenkirchen. Goalkeeper Ricardo was his team's hero, blocking spot-kicks from Frank Lampard, Steven Gerrard and Jamie Carragher to become the first man to save three penalties in a World Cup shoot-out. However, Portugal's luck ran out in the semi-finals when they lost 1-0 to France.

Eusebio celebrates a goal during the 1966 World Cup

PREVIOUS TOURNAMENTS

1930 Did not enter	1962 Did not qualify	1986 Round 1
1934 Did not qualify	1966 Third place	1990 Did not qualify
1938 Did not qualify	1970 Did not qualify	1994 Did not qualify
1950 Did not qualify	1974 Did not qualify	1998 Did not qualify
1954 Did not qualify	1978 Did not qualify	2002 Round 1
1958 Did not qualify	1982 Did not qualify	2006 Fourth place

SPAIN

So often derided as the great under-achievers of world football, Spain put all their past disappointments behind them when they won the 2008 European Championships in glorious style. That success, combined with their status as the best team in the world according to the FIFA rankings, has made Spain many people's favourites to triumph in South Africa this summer.

If anything, Spain's form during the World Cup qualifiers only added to the impression that this is a team at the very height of its formidable powers. Despite installing a new coach, Vicente del Bosque, at the start of the qualifying campaign, Spain merely took up where they left off in Switzerland and Austria during the Euros. Sweeping aside tricky opponents in Turkey, Bosnia and Belgium, they won all ten of their group games, scoring an impressive 28 goals in the process. Spain even managed to extend their unbeaten run to a record-equalling 35 matches, before losing 2-0 to the USA in the 2009 Confederations Cup semi-finals.

> **"We can't hide the fact that we are one of the favourites to win."**
> Spain coach Vicente del Bosque

That defeat may give their opponents some hope, but few would bet on the Spanish suffering a similar shock in South Africa. For a start, it's very difficult to even get the ball off Del Bosque's team, whose Barcelona-style possession game puts the opposition on the back foot from the start. Moreover, with the likes of Xavi, Iniesta and Xabi Alonso providing the ammunition and brilliant strikers Fernando Torres and David Villa firing the bullets, Spain have the ability to penetrate even the tightest of defences.

Their own defence, led by captain and shot-stopper supreme Iker Casillas, is sound enough, although occasionally vulnerable at set pieces. That, though, is a minor weakness in a side which has quality performers all over the pitch.

THE GAFFER: VICENTE DEL BOSQUE

Although he's only been in the job for less than two years, Vicente del Bosque already has an impressive record as the national coach of Spain. After taking over from the veteran Luis Aragones, who had led Spain to triumph in the 2008 European Championships, Del Bosque set a new world record by starting his reign with 13 straight victories. His record in the World Cup qualifying campaign was equally eye-catching, Spain running up ten wins out of ten in their group.

A dead ringer for Rene in the popular TV sitcom 'Allo 'Allo, the mustachioed Del Bosque was previously a long-term servant of Real Madrid, first as a defensive midfielder in the 1970s and 1980s. After retiring in 1984 he rose through the coaching ranks at the club before eventually becoming manager in 1999. His four years in the Bernabeu hotseat were extraordinarily successful, Real winning two Champions League titles and two league championships before Del Bosque was unceremoniously booted out just days after the second of these La Liga triumphs. After a brief spell with Besiktas he was linked with numerous national team jobs before being appointed Spain's coach in July 2008.

KEY PLAYER:
DAVID VILLA

A livewire striker who is deadly inside the penalty area, David Villa is the second highest goalscorer in Spain's history and is almost certain to break Raul's record of 44 goals for the national team in the near future.

Villa's football career, however, started unpromisingly when he was rejected by local club Real Oviedo for being too short. Instead he joined their Asturian rivals Sporting Gijon, before moving on to Real Zaragoza in 2003. Two years later he signed for his current club, Valencia, for around £9 million - a fee which proved to be a bargain as Villa developed a reputation as one of the most prolific strikers in Europe, topping the club's scoring charts every year and helping Valencia win the Copa del Rey in 2008. Since making his debut for Spain against San Marino in 2005 Villa has formed a superb partnership with Liverpool's Fernando Torres. The pair were instrumental in Spain's Euro 2008 success, Villa's four goals making him the tournament's leading scorer.

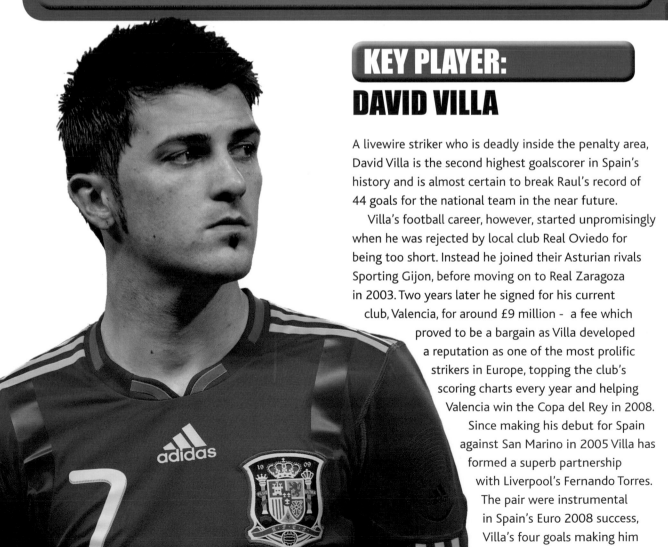

ONE TO WATCH: GERARD PIQUE

He may not play in all of his country's games at the World Cup but Barcelona defender Gerard Pique clearly has a big future ahead of him. A tall, physically imposing centre-back, Pique is dominant in the air but also has excellent skills on the ground and is quite capable of playing a more advanced role as a defensive midfielder.

A product of Barcelona's renowned youth system, Pique moved to Manchester United in 2004 but only featured occasionally at Old Trafford. After a loan spell at Real Zaragoza he returned to the Nou Camp in 2008, and the following year enjoyed an outstanding season as Barcelona became the first Spanish club to win the treble of league, Copa del Rey and Champions League – ironically, Barca's opponents in the final in this last competition were his old club, Manchester United.

Pique made his debut for Spain in a 2-0 friendly win against England in February 2009 and later went on to feature in three World Cup qualifiers. Still only 23, he will almost certainly be the central figure in Spain's defence for many years to come.

TACTICS BOARD: POSSESSION PLAY

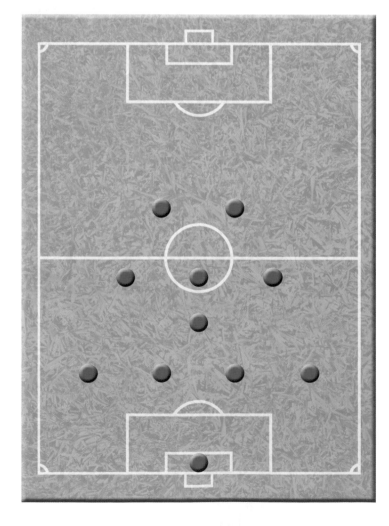

Spain's 4-1-3-2 formation provides the perfect platform for their main strategic aim: taking control of the middle of the pitch, where their trademark short passing style can be most effective in launching attacks on their opponents' goal.

It helps, of course, that Spain have technically brilliant players in midfield who rarely give the ball away, enabling the team to almost set up camp in the opposition half. The metronomic passing of the Barcelona pair Xavi and Andres Iniesta is central to Spain's build-up play, although the importance of holding midfielder Xabi Alonso should not be under-estimated. As well as starting the attacking process by taking possession from centre backs Carlos Puyol and Gerard Pique, the former Liverpool star has the ability to hit pinpoint longer passes forwards to strike partners David Villa and Fernando Torres, or out wide to attacking midfielder David Silva or marauding full backs Sergio Ramos and Joan Capdevila.

SPAIN AT THE WORLD CUP

• Spain got off to a great start at their first World Cup in 1934, beating Brazil 3-1 in the first round. Their next game with hosts Italy went to a replay, but the Spanish were depleted by injuries and lost 1-0.

• **Spain had better luck at the 1950 tournament in Brazil when they won all three of their group games against USA, Chile and England to make it into a final pool of four teams. After an encouraging 2-2 draw with eventual winners Uruguay, though, Spain were thrashed 6-1 by Brazil and 3-1 by Sweden to finish fourth.**

• Despite Real Madrid's domination of the European Cup in its early years, Spain surprisingly made little impression in the World Cups of the late 1950s and early 1960s. The Spanish failed to qualify for the 1958 tournament, and went home after the group stage in 1962 in Chile. It was the same story in 1966, as Spain left the finals in England after collecting just two points from their three games.

• **As hosts in 1982 Spain fared somewhat better, but didn't exactly cover themselves in glory either. After sneaking through the group stage despite a humiliating loss to Northern Ireland in Madrid,**

Spanish midfielder Sergi plays against Italy at the 1994 World Cup

Spain battled it out with West Germany and England in a second group stage for a place in the semi-finals. Sadly for the home fans, they could only manage a single point and were eliminated.

• Four years later Spain produced a superb performance to beat Denmark 5-1 in the last 16 in Mexico, Real Madrid striker Emilio 'The Vulture' Butragueno scoring four of the goals. Inconsistent as ever, though, the Spanish lost out to Belgium in the quarter-finals.

• **Since then, the Spanish have made it to the quarter-finals on two more occasions, narrowly**

losing to Italy in 1994 and host nation South Korea on penalties in 2002. Both of these defeats were slightly unfortunate: in the first game, Spain's Luis Enrique should have been awarded a penalty when he was clearly elbowed by an Italian defender; in the second game, Spain were denied two apparently valid goals by the officials.

• However legitimate these complaints may be, there is no denying that Spain have a pretty poor World Cup record. As one of the favourites in South Africa the Spanish will be desperately hoping that these past failures do not come back to haunt them at this summer's finals.

PREVIOUS TOURNAMENTS

1930 Did not enter	1962 Round 1	1986 Quarter-finals
1934 Quarter-finals	1966 Round 1	1990 Round 2
1938 Did not enter	1970 Did not qualify	1994 Quarter-finals
1950 Fourth place	1974 Did not qualify	1998 Round 1
1954 Did not qualify	1978 Round 1	2002 Quarter-finals
1958 Did not qualify	1982 Round 2	2006 Round 2

SWITZERLAND

Switzerland may not be the most glamorous of the teams appearing in South Africa but in manager Ottmar Hitzfeld, the former boss of Bayern Munich and Borussia Dortmund, they have one of the most well-known faces in world football. What's more, 'Der General', as he is dubbed, is a master tactician who will make the Swiss extremely difficult to beat.

A two-time winner of the Champions League, Hitzfeld was appointed Switzerland manager in 2008. His reign started poorly, though, with a shock 2-1 home defeat to Luxembourg that threatened to derail their World Cup qualifying bid from the off, but an eight-match unbeaten run put them back on track and they eventually claimed top spot in their group ahead of Greece with a 0-0 draw at home to Israel.

> "We have been given a hard but approachable group. Things could have been worse."
>
> Switzerland coach Ottmar Hitzfeld

Under Hitzfeld, Switzerland generally play a 4-4-2 system with the emphasis on fast counter-attacks instigated by star player Tranquillo Barnetta. Defensively the Swiss are solid, particularly in the middle where the Arsenal duo of Philippe Senderos and Johan Djourou form a strong partnership. Behind them, goalkeeper Diego Benaglio is a capable performer, currently enjoying the best years of his career with 2009 Bundesliga champions Wolfsburg. However, Benaglio and co. will have to go some to match the Swiss' feat at the last World Cup when they didn't concede a single goal in their four games.

Up front, meanwhile, Switzerland have a couple of veteran strikers in 30-year-old Alexander Frei, his country's all-time leading scorer with 40 goals, and 34-year-old Blaise Nkufo, a Zaire-born forward with Steve McClaren's FC Twente who scored five goals in the qualifying round.

If those two can defy the years to find the target regularly and their defence stays firm, Switzerland will have every chance of making it into the knock-out phase.

SWITZERLAND AT THE WORLD CUP

• Switzerland first competed at the World Cup in Italy in 1934. Their centre forward Poldi Kielholz wore spectacles both on and off the pitch, but they didn't stop him from scoring three goals as the Swiss advanced to the quarter-finals before losing to Czechoslovakia.

• The Swiss reached the quarter-finals again in 1938 and, for a third time, as hosts in 1954 when they were beaten 7-5 by Austria in the highest-scoring World Cup finals match ever.

• In 2006 Switzerland became the first ever team to be knocked out of the World Cup without conceding a single goal. After a 0-0 draw with France, the Swiss beat both Togo and South Korea 2-0 to advance to the knock-out stage.

• In the last 16 Switzerland drew 0-0 with Ukraine, but then lost 3-0 on penalties – the first time in World Cup history that a team had failed to score in a shoot-out. Ironically, these were the first penalties the Swiss had taken at the World Cup as they had not been awarded a regular spot-kick in their previous 26 matches.

PREVIOUS TOURNAMENTS

1930 Did not enter	1962 Round 1	1986 Did not qualify
1934 Quarter-finals	1966 Round 1	1990 Did not qualify
1938 Quarter-finals	1970 Did not qualify	1994 Round 2
1950 Round 1	1974 Did not qualify	1998 Did not qualify
1954 Quarter-finals	1978 Did not qualify	2002 Did not qualify
1958 Did not qualify	1982 Did not qualify	2006 Round 2

KEY PLAYER:
TRANQUILLO BARNETTA

A talented winger who can also play in a defensive midfield role, Tranquillo Barnetta provides a touch of the unexpected in a Switzerland side which is otherwise lacking in flair.

Great things have been expected of the 24-year-old since he helped the Swiss win the Under-17 European Championship in 2002. Two years later he won his first full cap and he has now played more than 40 times for his country, including some eye-catching displays at the last World Cup which led to him being short-listed for the tournament's Best Young Player award.

Barnetta began his club career with Swiss side St Gallen before moving to German giants Bayer Leverkusen in 2004. He initially spent a short spell on loan at Hannover before returning to establish himself in the Bayer line up.

HONDURAS

Simply having qualified for the World Cup is a great achievement for Honduras, who have only appeared once before at the finals – back in 1982. Underdogs they may be, but the Central Americans have a team full of experience and they will give all their opponents a run for their money in South Africa.

Honduras finished third in their qualifying group behind the USA and Mexico and level on points with Costa Rica, whose inferior goal difference condemned them to a play-off against Uruguay, which they subsequently lost. The Hondurans' success was largely based on a strong defence which conceded just 11 goals in 10 matches – the best record in their group.

Goalkeeper Noel Valladares, though, did not have the best of campaigns and his occasional mistakes earned much criticism from the local media. He is likely, though, to retain his place at the finals in a defence which also features Wigan left-back Maynor Figueroa. In midfield, meanwhile, Honduras have a number of highly capable performers including the combative Wilson Palacios, Parma free-kick specialist Julio Cesar de Leon, and Toronto's Amado Guevara, a skilful technician who has accumulated a record 130 caps for his country.

Honduras' Colombian coach Reinaldo Reina alternates between a 4-4-2 system and a more defensive 4-5-1 formation, so it remains to be seen whether he opts for a lone striker or, as most fans would prefer, sends out both his main attackers, 36-year-old warhorse Carlos Pavon, his country's all-time leading scorer with nearly 60 international goals to his name, and the speedy David Suazo, a bit-part player with Inter Milan.

Certainly, Honduras will need to score goals as their defence, however efficient in the qualifiers, is unlikely to keep out Torres and co.

> **"There's no question that playing abroad has given Honduran players something extra. They've got belief in their ability and their self-confidence has increased."**
>
> Honduras coach
> Reinaldo Rueda

HONDURAS AT THE WORLD CUP

• Honduras were involved in the most violent episode in World Cup history when a series of three qualifying matches against neighbours El Salvador in 1969 inflamed already existing tensions between the two countries to such an extent that a four-day war broke out. Around 3,000 people lost their lives in the so-called 'Soccer War' before international pressure led to a ceasefire.

• **Honduras reached the World Cup finals for the first time in 1982. The Central Americans surpassed expectations, drawing 1-1 with hosts Spain in their opening match before holding Northern Ireland to another 1-1 draw five days later.**

• Going into their final match against Yugoslavia, Honduras knew they needed at least a point to stand a chance of progressing to the next round. For most of the match they seemed likely to get it, until a late penalty ended their dream.

• **Back in Honduras, though, the fans were just pleased that their team had done much better than the hated Salvadoreans, whose 10-1 defeat by Hungary was the biggest drubbing in World Cup history.**

PREVIOUS TOURNAMENTS

1930 Did not enter	1962 Did not qualify	1986 Did not qualify
1934 Did not enter	1966 Did not qualify	1990 Did not qualify
1938 Did not enter	1970 Did not qualify	1994 Did not qualify
1950 Did not enter	1974 Did not qualify	1998 Did not qualify
1954 Did not enter	1978 Withdrew	2002 Did not qualify
1958 Did not enter	1982 Round 1	2006 Did not qualify

KEY PLAYER: WILSON PALACIOS

Despite being aged just 25, Wilson Palacios already has nearly 70 caps for his country and his experience will be vital to Honduras in South Africa. A powerful midfielder who was once likened by his former manager Steve Bruce to 'a young Paul Ince', Palacios first arrived in England from Honduran club Olimpia in 2007. He had a trial with Arsenal, before playing on loan for Birmingham and then finally made a permanent move to Wigan. His impressive performances for the Latics soon sparked interest from bigger Premiership clubs, and in January 2009 he joined Tottenham for £12 million.

However, an apparent success story also has its tragic side. In 2007 Palacios' 16-year-old brother Edwin was kidnapped by a gang in Honduras and, although the family paid a ransom, the youngster was murdered two years later.

CHILE

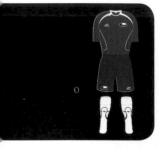

If Chile can show something of the form they produced in their qualifying campaign then they will provide highly entertaining viewing at the World Cup. With just one point and one goal less than group winners Brazil, Chile were runners-up in the South American section and earned many plaudits for the positive way they played both home and away.

Chilean coach since 2007, Marcelo Bielsa has fast-tracked a group of talented young players into the national team and encouraged them to attack whenever possible. Their results have been outstanding, none more so than a thrilling 4-2 victory in Colombia which clinched Chile's place in the finals. Bielsa, though, will be wary of adding to the hype surrounding the team, having been scarred by the experience of leading his native Argentina to an ignominious first-round exit at the 2002 finals.

However, Chile certainly have enough quality to reach the knock-out stages. Although the team boasts few star names, it has a strong work ethic and there are classy performers in every area of the field. The key figures in defence are goalkeeper and captain Claudio Bravo, who plays for Real Sociedad, and veteran central defender Pablo Contreras of Greek side PAOK. The highly rated Matias Fernandez of Sporting Lisbon is the main creative force in midfield, while in attack the prolific Humberto Suazo is a one-man goalscoring machine. Suazo is usually supported by two tricky wingers in an offensive-minded 4-3-3 formation: 21-year-old Alexis 'The Wonder Boy' Sanchez of Udinese and Mark 'Speedy' Gonzalez, who was briefly on Liverpool's books and now plays for CSKA Moscow.

Chile probably won't win the World Cup but they could pull off a shock or two, and however they fare their attacking philosophy is sure to earn them new admirers.

> **"I feel good when my teams spend more time attacking than defending."**
> Chile coach
> Marcelo Bielsa

CHILE AT THE WORLD CUP

• By far Chile's best performance at the World Cup was as hosts in 1962. In a bizarre pre-match ritual, the team ate Swiss cheese before beating Switzerland, spaghetti before beating Italy and drank vodka before beating the Soviet Union. Before their semi-final against Brazil the Chileans drank coffee, but it did them little good as they went on to lose 4-2.

• **Chile were thrown out of the 1990 World Cup after their goalkeeper Roberto Rojas feigned injury when a firecracker was thrown near him during a qualifier against Brazil. Believing that Rojas had been hurt the referee abandoned the game, but FIFA later awarded Brazil a 2-0 victory. As a further punishment Chile were excluded altogether from the 1994 tournament.**

• The South Americans bounced back to qualify for the 1998 finals in France, where they were the only team to reach the second round despite not winning a single match, three draws proving sufficient for second place in the group. Brazil soon ended their World Cup dream, though, winning 4-1 in the last 16.

PREVIOUS TOURNAMENTS

1930 Round 1	1962 Third place	1986 Did not qualify
1934 Withdrew	1966 Round 1	1990 Disqualified
1938 Withdrew	1970 Did not qualify	1994 Banned
1950 Round 1	1974 Round 1	1998 Round 2
1954 Did not qualify	1978 Did not qualify	2002 Did not qualify
1958 Did not qualify	1982 Round 1	2006 Did not qualify

KEY PLAYER:
HUMBERTO SUAZO

Chile's successful World Cup qualifying campaign owed a lot to Humberto Suazo. The 28-year-old striker's tally of 10 goals made him the top scorer in the South American section – one ahead of Brazil's Luis Fabiano – and marked him out as a player to watch at the finals in South Africa.

Suazo, who now plays for Mexican side Monterrey having previously won three Chilean league titles with Colo-Colo, is a lethal finisher with good close control, but has a notoriously short fuse which has landed him in trouble on numerous occasions.

However, if he can keep his temper in check this summer he should have a good World Cup, in which case he may well land the move he craves to a major European club.

GIANLUIGI BUFFON

It is not often that a goalkeeper's name is spoken in the same breath as match-winning strikers and talented playmakers but that merely shows the esteem in which Italian stopper Gianluigi Buffon is held within the world game. The Italy number one is generally regarded as the best goalkeeper on planet football on account of his razor-sharp reflexes, confident catching and incredible presence between the posts.

Juventus certainly thought so when they paid £23million back in the summer of 2001 – a world record fee for a goalkeeper – to prise him away from his hometown club, Parma, with whom he made his Serie A debut as a 17-year-old in 1995. In many ways it's no surprise that Buffon made a career for himself in the sporting domain – his mother was a discus thrower of some renown in Italy, while his father was a celebrated weightlifter. Young Gianluigi, however, was happy to stick with football and he has enjoyed an illustrious career, the highlight of which was undoubtedly Italy's World Cup triumph in 2006.

World Cups are generally remembered for great goals and flashes of individual brilliance but Buffon and his defence earned many headlines four years ago in Germany. They went a full 457 minutes without conceding a goal between their second group game against the USA right through to the final against France, when Zinedine Zidane slotted home an early penalty. Italy eventually went on to win that game on penalties but an extraordinary save in extra-time from a Zidane header ensured that the Azzurri were able to take the game to spot-kicks.

Buffon was in top form once again during Italy's qualifying campaign for the 2010 World Cup, and he has even taken to wearing the captain's armband when Fabio Cannavaro has been absent through injury. At 32, Buffon's form is as good as it ever was and there's every chance that this tournament in South Africa won't be his last.

Buffon went 457 minutes without conceding a goal at the last World Cup

STATS

DOB: 28 January 1978
International Debut: v Russia, 29 October 1997
Caps: 100
Goals: 0
World Cup finals appearances: 2002, 2006 (11 apps)
World Cup finals goals: 0

DIDIER DROGBA

When it comes to doing something worthwhile for his country, there's no doubt that Didier Drogba's greatest feat has come off the pitch rather than on it. Back in 2005, moments after the Ivory Coast had guaranteed their participation at a World Cup finals for the first time, Drogba grabbed a microphone in the dressing-room and went down on his hands and knees to beg the leaders on both sides of the country's brutal civil war to lay down their arms.

Within a couple of days, both factions had called a ceasefire so it is not difficult to understand why Drogba is viewed as a hero in his native land. "I have won many trophies in my time," says the man himself, "but nothing will ever top helping win the battle for peace in my country."

Drogba the peacemaker may be a difficult image to swallow for millions of football fans the world over who have watched the 32-year-old chase referees and scream obscenities at television cameras in the past, but if you put Drogba's many faults to one side for a moment, there's no argument that he's one hell of a player.

He arrived at Chelsea in July 2004 via Le Mans, Guingamp and Marseille and immediately began to justify his £24million price tag. Physically, there might be a few better-built centre forwards in the world but few possess the subtlety of touch and finishing ability of the Ivorian. Unfortunately, the 2006 World Cup only got a brief glimpse of a semi-fit Drogba and his side were eliminated in the group stages but this time around he is expecting better things from both himself and his team.

Drogba has even suggested that the Ivory Coast have the ability within their ranks to make it as far as the business end of the tournament. "To make it to the final will not be easy because there are great teams like Brazil and Germany who have won the World Cup for many years," he says. "But my team-mates and I want to make history and want to change the way the world sees African football. I hope that we'll be the team that is going to go to the final and win the competition."

Didier Drogba - goalscorer and peacemaker

STATS

DOB: 11 March 1978
International Debut: v South Africa, 8 September 2002
Caps: 60
Goals: 41
World Cup finals appearances: 2006 (2 apps)
World Cup finals goals: 1

SAMUEL ETO'O

If it seems as though Samuel Eto'o has been around forever, it might just be because he has. He made his international debut for Cameroon the day before his 16th birthday and now, at the ripe old age of 29, he will be playing in his third World Cup finals. His previous two efforts – where Cameroon have been eliminated each time at the group stage – have been far from impressive, but Eto'o has already won two African Nations Cup titles with the Indomitable Lions, while he was also part of the side that won Olympic football gold in Sydney in 2000.

At club level, too, Eto'o has amassed plenty of honours. He was first brought to Spain by Real Madrid, who sold him onto Mallorca before Barcelona became impressed by his strength on the ball and eye for goal in the summer of 2004. At the Nou Camp, the player notched 108 goals in 145 matches and played his part in three La Liga title wins, as well as two European Cup successes. Now at Inter Milan following a £40million transfer last summer, Eto'o is the most decorated African player on the planet and his nine goals in 11 qualifiers were significant in Cameroon earning World Cup qualification again after they missed out on the 2006 tournament in Germany.

There's no doubt that this fiery character will be pumped up for the tournament. Thumb through the statistics in Eto'o's career and it doesn't take long to realise that the World Cup finals is the one stage where he has so far failed to perform. This summer he'll be hoping to make up for those previous disappointments by leading his team out of their group for the first time since the 1990 World Cup in Italy. "We have again made people believe in this team," he says. "It's a great achievement for all of us to be able to play in a World Cup, especially one in Africa. We are dangerous because we have a good mix of experience, and we have learned to play together."

Eto'o will be hoping to improve on his record of one World Cup goal in two tournaments

STATS

DOB: 10 March 1981
International Debut: v Costa Rica, 9 March 1997
Caps: 87
Goals: 42
World Cup finals appearances: 1998, 2002 (4 apps)
World Cup finals goals: 1

KAKA

In the eyes of most Brazilians, Kaka's innate football abilities on the pitch make him a God-like figure but the player himself doesn't buy into such comparisons. As a devout Christian, Kaka (born Ricardo Izecson dos Santos Leite) isn't impressed by such throwaway remarks and when you hear his story you can understand why.

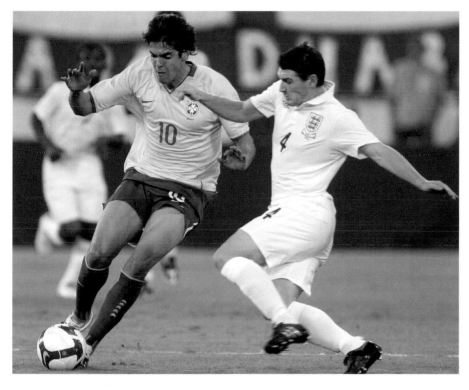

Kaka will be hoping his World Cup experience this summer is more like 2002 than 2006

together, tying up one move and starting another.

This summer in South Africa will be Kaka's third World Cup and he'll be hoping it will be more like the 2002 experience, where Brazil emerged winners, rather than the 2006 version where they were sent packing in the quarter-finals.

"The World Cup is massive for everyone, everyone wants to be there, but especially for Brazilians," he points out. "We have made a big sacrifice to qualify. It is not so easy for us, most of whom play in Europe, to go to South America for the qualifying matches. But all of us enjoy representing our country and we know our responsibility from now on. After the qualification, the pressure only gets bigger."

With God on his side, he's sure to cope.

As a youngster Kaka was almost paralysed when he fractured his spine jumping into a swimming pool, and he has put his subsequent recovery down to the man above. As a thank you, he now pays a regular percentage of his income to the church, as well as praying openly on the pitch when Brazil win and donning an 'I belong to Jesus' t-shirt under his shirt.

In football terms, Kaka belongs to Real Madrid who bought him from Milan for a fee of £55million and it's easy to understand why they stumped up so much cash. Kaka is the best player in the world at operating 'in the hole' behind the strikers, in fact he alone probably defines the role. He may not catch the eye as regularly as some of his Madrid or Brazilian teammates, but he is the one linking play

STATS

DOB: 22 April 1982
International Debut: v Bolivia, 31 Jan 2002
Caps: 73
Goals: 26
World Cup finals appearances: 2002, 2006
World Cup finals goals: 1

THIERRY HENRY

Rarely has a player at a World Cup been under so much scrutiny. Because of the contribution of his left hand to France's play-off victory over Ireland in November, Thierry Henry's actions will be under close analysis every time he controls the ball or goes down under a challenge from an opponent. There are some who say he shouldn't be allowed play in South Africa at all this summer, and his critics won't be slow to echo that point if his behaviour is anything other than impeccable.

In some ways it's unfortunate because Henry's fourth appearance at the World Cup should be a celebration, not an examination. The 32-year-old striker has had a long and fruitful relationship with the tournament, one that started back in 1998 when he was part of the French team that won the World Cup on home soil. Henry, who played as a right-winger back then, scored three goals in the tournament to help France to victory but he was an unused substitute in the final and never got to break sweat on one of his country's most memorable nights. When France lost to Italy in the 2006 final on penalties, Henry was also off the pitch, due to injury this time, and he'll no doubt be keen to made a significant contribution in a final this time around.

That, of course, might be a far-fetched idea given the current troubles in the French camp. Henry, as team captain, has had regular arguments with coach Raymond Domenech over the past 12 months and it would seem that these two will have to come to some sort of professional understanding if France are to prosper in South Africa.

As for Henry himself, he'll most likely play on the left side of a three-pronged French attack in these finals, a position he has played for Barcelona over the past two seasons, and if he can link successfully with the likes of Franck Ribery, Nicolas Anelka and Karim Benzema – and the captain and manager can sort out their differences – France are capable of beating any side in the tournament.

Henry will want to do the talking with his feet, not his left hand, in South Africa

STATS

DOB: 17 August 1977
International Debut: v South Africa, 11 October 1997
Caps: 117
Goals: 51
World Cup finals appearances: 1998, 2002, 2006 (15 apps)
World Cup finals goals: 6

LIONEL MESSI

Lionel Messi has been compared to Diego Maradona his whole life, but the diminutive Argentinean didn't pull on his hero's famous number ten shirt for the first time until the great man himself took charge of the national team in March 2009.

Messi now feels at home in Argentina's famous number 10 shirt

Before then, the little genius had been afraid to put himself in direct comparison with one the greatest footballers who ever lived. He need not have been so shy. The 22-year-old appears to possess many of the same abilities – most notably a cultured left boot and a similar low centre of gravity – as his famous mentor, now manager, once did and all he needs now is a strong World Cup showing to prove it. Messi did play back in the 2006 World Cup in Germany but Argentina's quarter-final exit denied him the opportunity to peddle his impressive wares on the world's greatest stage.

We have, though, already seen most of his repertoire for Barcelona over the past few years. Despite his age, Messi has already won three La Liga titles and two European Cups with the Catalan club and yet there were times during his youth career when experts felt the player would never make it. As a youngster with Newell's Old Boys in his native land, Messi was diagnosed with a growth hormone deficiency and he

was forced to undergo expensive nightly injections for four years to correct the problem.

His five foot six inch frame still might not be the most imposing in the world game but Messi remains an incredible talent from whom it is virtually impossible to steal the ball. "Leo simply goes one way with his body and another with the ball," says Barcelona and Spain centre-half Gerard Piqué. "You have to either guess right or foul him." Messi receiving the ball from a teammate with his back to goal and swiveling past a defender breathing down his neck has become one of the most enjoyable parts of watching a great Barcelona team play.

The same logic can apply to Argentina if Messi can link up successfully with the likes of Sergio Aguero, Gonzalo Higuain and Carlos Tevez in Argentina's quality attack.

STEVEN PIENAAR

To play in the opening match of a World Cup is a special moment for any player, but it might be a little more memorable for Steven Pienaar when he walks out at the Soccer City Stadium in Johannesburg for South Africa's game against Mexico on June 11. "Not far from where my mother lives you can actually see the stadium," says Pienaar. "I used to dream of playing in the old stadium, so to play in this new one that is something very special for me."

When Pienaar does take the pitch for that game, he will be the player all of South Africa expects to make a difference. While the 28-year-old is generally used as a wide midfielder by David Moyes at Everton, he lines up as a central playmaker for his country. In a side that is largely inexperienced on the international stage, Pienaar is the man who sets South Africa's tempo and generally runs the show.

His rise from the townships of Johannesburg to Merseyside hasn't been straightforward. Having come through the youth ranks at Dutch club Breda, he was then signed by Ajax and won two titles with the famous club before moving on to Borussia Dortmund. However, he was unable to settle in Germany and that's when Everton became interested.

Since moving to Goodison Park in the summer of 2007, Pienaar has stepped up another level as a footballer and every last ounce of his talent will be needed this summer if his country are to avoid the embarrassment of exiting the tournament in the group stages. There has even been a campaign in recent months to make Pienaar, and not Portsmouth's Aaron Mokoena's, the Bafana Bafana captain for the tournament but the player himself might be better without the responsibility. There's going to be enough pressure on his shoulders as it is.

Pienaar grew up in the shadow of the Soccer City Stadium in Johannesburg

STATS

DOB: 17 March 1982
International Debut: v Turkey, 23 May 2002
Caps: 43
Goals: 2
World Cup finals appearances: 0
World Cup finals goals: 0

CRISTIANO RONALDO

The most expensive footballer on the planet didn't exactly cover himself in glory at the last World Cup. The most memorable image of the Portuguese star from Germany 2006 was of him winking at his own bench after playing his part in getting Wayne Rooney sent off in his country's quarter-final against England.

Portugal went on to get knocked out by France at the semi-final stage but since that defeat in Munich, Ronaldo's career has really taken off. While playing for Manchester United in 2007/08, the winger scored an incredible 42 goals in 49 appearances as his side won the Premier League and European Cup. Ronaldo was simply mesmeric that season, with his torpedo-like free-kicks from distance becoming something of a trademark as he won United game after game, virtually single-handed. His transfer to Real Madrid in the summer of 2009, for a world record fee of £80million, was a blow to his old club, but he has started life at the Bernabeu with the same tricks, flicks and free-kicks that he regularly displayed at Old Trafford.

An early season injury suffered with his new club forced him to miss the two legs of Portugal's play-off victory over Bosnia-Herzegovina, which ensured the country's presence at June's World Cup, but the 2008 Ballon D'Or and FIFA World Player of the Year winner will have to step up to the mark if Carlos Queiroz's side are to repeat their impressive efforts at the last World Cup. In particular, Portugal will be hoping that Ronaldo can make some impact on the scoring front, and there is some belief that Queiroz will shift him from the wing to a more central role for the tournament, where he will most likely attempt to forge a partnership with Liedson, Sporting Lisbon's Brazilian born striker who became eligible to play for Portugal in August 2009.

Even with that help, though, Ronaldo will be carrying the team on his shoulders.

The world's most expensive footballer will be central to Portugal's hopes in South Africa

STATS

DOB: 5 February 1985
International Debut: v Kazakhstan,
   20 August 2003
Caps: 68
Goals: 22
World Cup finals appearances: 2006 (6 apps)
World Cup finals goals: 1

WAYNE ROONEY

Is South Africa 2010 going to be the stage where Wayne Rooney makes an indelible mark on the world game, forging his place forever amongst the list of football greats? England's talismanic striker certainly has that potential.

Rooney has already buried the demons of Germany 2006 when his moment of madness – the petulant stamp on Ricardo Cavalho – arguably cost his country a place in the semi-finals. Since then he has matured, both as a footballer and a man. The dark side to his temper, not the positive side that makes him such an eager competitor, appears to have vanished. Rooney still possess a manic desire for the game but these days – thanks to the influence of two of the world's great managers, Alex Ferguson and Fabio Capello – it is controlled. In short he has grown up, both on the pitch and off it and in 2009 he captained England against Brazil within weeks of becoming a father.

No part of Rooney's game is lacking. He can find a teammate with an incisive pass, dribble past three or four defenders and finish like a true goal poacher too – be it finishing off a move from inside the six yard box or smashing one home from 30 yards out – and he has become central to the working of Capello's England team operating in a free role, usually behind Emile Heskey.

Rooney will also be grimly determined to put one statistic right this summer. The boy from the blue half of Liverpool has always scored goals, and plenty of them, but heading into the summer's tournament he won't be too happy to see a big fat nought beside his name when it comes to World Cup goals. Just watch, he'll be itching to right that particular wrong every second he's on the pitch in South Africa.

Wayne Rooney has become England's main man

STATS

DOB: 24 October 1985
International Debut: v Australia,
  12 February 2003
Caps: 55
Goals: 25
World Cup finals appearances: 2006 (4 apps)
World Cup finals goals: 0

FERNANDO TORRES

The South African soil seems to agree with Fernando Torres. In a Confederations Cup game against New Zealand at the Royal Bafokeng Stadium in Rustenburg last June, Il Nino notched a hat-trick in just 11 first-half minutes, a record for a Spanish footballer. Nobody would be surprised if he were to replicate that feat this summer, particularly as he'll be serviced by a Spanish midfield that is arguably the best in the business.

But even without those clever operators behind him, Torres is the kind of player capable of creating something from nothing, as Liverpool supporters can bear testament to. He is among the fastest strikers over ten yards on the planet, and in the past few seasons he has added a physical strength to his repetoire that wasn't evident when he first made a name for himself as a teenager at Atletico Madrid.

Few players of his age have such big tournament experience – Torres has played at Euro 2004 and 2008, as well as the 2006 World Cup – but it is the most recent tournament that he will remember fondest. Initially, things didn't go too well for him in Austria and Switzerland - he was substituted on a number of occasions by Spanish manager Luis Aragones in his side's early games - but Torres eventually proved that his worth to the veteran manager and popped up with an 33rd minute goal in the final against Germany to win the European Championships for Spain.

Since then, Torres has been largely absent in a Spanish shirt due to a series of groin injuries but the World Cup has never been far from his mind. "If I can touch the cup it will be the best moment for a footballer," he says. "After that you cannot do anything better. But there is high expectation for us, and that is not always the best for you, that pressure. I think you have one chance in your life to win the World Cup and maybe this is our chance. We have good players, playing well together, who have been together for three, four years. If we miss this chance, this may be it."

Fernando Torres will be hoping to fire Spain to World Cup glory this summer

NEMANJA VIDIC

Tall, well-built and skin-headed, Serbia's, Nemanja Vidic looks every inch the no-nonsense defender and while he does all his primary defensive duties in a straightforward manner, the statistics about his game reveal a surprise or two. While Rio Ferdinand is generally proclaimed to be the best passer of Manchester United's two centre-halves, the numbers show that Vidic is actually more accurate with his distribution than the England international, over both long and short distances.

Overall, he's a class act and a player who has contributed significantly to his country's cause down the years. In the qualifying campaign for the 2006 World Cup – when Serbia and Montenegro were united – Vidic was part of a back four who conceded just one goal in ten qualifying games. They weren't as mean in winning qualifying group seven ahead of France this time around but eight goals conceded in ten games was still a pretty impressive tally. Vidic and his centre-half partner for Serbia, the imposing Aleksander Lukovic of Udinese, will not be beaten easily.

In June, Vidic will look to make up for what was a horrible World Cup experience in 2006. To start with, the centre-half was ruled out of Serbia's first group game against Holland through a suspension picked up in the qualifying campaign and then, while training in advance of Serbia and Montenegro's match against Argentina, he tore the ligaments in his left knee, ruling him out of the rest of the tournament.

It was a blow to the player but since that disappointment three summer's ago, Vidic has gone on the prove himself one of the best defenders in the game with his assured displays for Manchester United in the Premier League and Champions League. When the 28-year-old does finally make his World Cup bow in June, not one centre forward in the entire tournament will look forward to facing him.

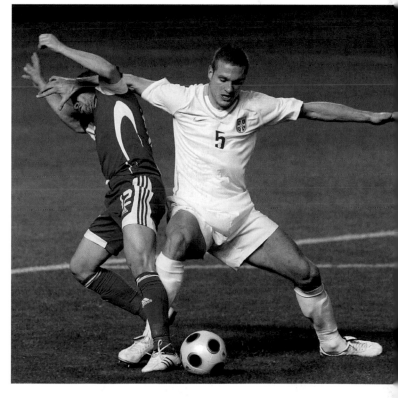

Few strikers will look forward to face the imposing Nemanja Vidic in South Africa

STATS

DOB: 21 October 1981
International Debut: v Italy, 12 October 2002
Caps: 44
Goals: 2
World Cup finals appearances: 0
World Cup finals goals: 0

WORLD CUP HISTORY

The idea of a world football championship was first raised at FIFA's inaugural meeting in Paris in 1904, but only really gained momentum in the 1920s. A proposal to hold a World Cup tournament was agreed in 1928 in Amsterdam, with Uruguay's bid to act as the host nation being accepted the following year. Since then the World Cup finals have been played 18 times, and seven nations have gone on to lift one of the two trophies (Brazil got to keep the first after winning their third tournament in 1970, although it was subsequently stolen and never seen again!).

1930, URUGUAY

Of the 13 countries who arrived in Montevideo in July 1930 only four made the three week boat journey from Europe. Among the absentees were the four Home Nations, who had resigned from FIFA following an argument about payments to amateur players. Germany, Spain and Italy also stayed at home, leaving just France, Belgium, Romania and Yugoslavia to fly the flag for Europe.

The original World Cup, the Jules Rimet Trophy

Of that quartet only Yugoslavia won their group, after victories against Brazil and Bolivia, to reach the semi-final where they were duly crushed 6-1 by the hosts. The next day, Argentina beat the USA by the same score to join Uruguay in the final.

Although Uruguay had the advantage of playing at home, thousands of Argentinean fans made the journey across the River Plate to support their team. The recently constructed Centenary Stadium in Montevideo was packed with 93,000 fans two hours before kick-off, while behind the scenes the teams argued about which ball to use. Eventually FIFA settled the dispute by ruling that the two countries could use their preferred ball for a half each.

Playing with their opponents' ball, Uruguay took an early lead, but Argentina hit back with two goals before half-time to stun the home fans into silence. The hosts, though, dominated after the break and soon equalised through inside forward Pedro Cea. Ten minutes later left-winger Santos Iriarte restored Uruguay's lead before centre-forward Hector Castro wrapped up his side's victory in the closing seconds.

As Uruguay captain Jose Nasazzi was presented with the gold cup by FIFA President Jules Rimet, motor horns blared in the streets of Montevideo while the ships sounded their sirens in the port. Despite the disappointing turnout from Europe, the first World Cup had been a huge success.

1934, ITALY

By 1934 the World Cup was already starting to expand. No fewer than 32 countries entered the qualifying competition, with half of that number reaching the finals in Italy. For the only time in the history of the tournament the holders, Uruguay, still bitter about being snubbed by the main European powers four years earlier, declined to defend their trophy. Again, the Home Nations stayed away, the FA's dismissive attitude towards the World Cup being summed up by committee member Charles Sutcliffe, who said: "The national associations of England, Scotland, Wales and Ireland have quite enough to do in their own International Championship which seems to me a far better World Championship than the one to be staged in Rome."

This time the tournament was organised on a straight knock-out basis, with the two South American representatives, Argentina and Brazil, falling at the first hurdle to Sweden and Spain respectively. Neither of the

The Italian team before the 1934 World Cup final

victors, though, survived the second round, leaving Czechoslovakia, Germany, Austria and Italy to battle it out in the semi-finals. In Milan, the hosts beat the Austrians thanks to a single goal by right-winger Enrique Guaita, one of three former Argentinean internationals in the Italian team. On the same day in Rome, Italian dictator Benito Mussolini watched Czechoslovakia defeat Germany 3-1.

The final, played in front of 45,000 fans at the Stadio Nazionale in Rome, was a tight affair. The Czechs' attractive short-passing game was eventually rewarded twenty minutes from the end when left-winger Antonin Puc scored with a long-range effort after his corner had only partially been cleared. Italy nearly fell two behind when a Czech effort hit the post, but made the most of their luck to equalise through a crazily swerving shot by left-winger Raimundo Orsi, another Argentine, with just eight minutes to play. The match moved into extra-time, centre forward Angelo Schiavio grabbing the winner for Italy early in the first period after being set up by Guaita.

1938, FRANCE

It was, perhaps, fitting that the third World Cup was held in France in 1938 as two Frenchmen, FIFA President Jules Rimet and Henri Delaunay, Secretary of the French FA, had been instrumental in setting up the competition a decade earlier.

For a second time the tournament followed a knock-out pattern, Brazil's incredible 6-5 defeat of Poland the pick of the first round matches. Two of the ties went to replays, Cuba surprisingly beating Romania and Germany going down to Switzerland despite holding a 2-0 lead at half-time. The Cubans, though, were trounced 8-0 by Sweden in the second round, while Switzerland were eliminated by Hungary, who went on to crush the Swedes 5-1 in the semi-final in Paris. In the other half of the draw, a violent encounter between Brazil and Czechoslovakia produced two broken limbs and three expulsions, and was only settled in the South Americans' favour after a replay. Brazil's World Cup, however, ended when they were beaten 2-1 in the semi-final by holders Italy, who had earlier accounted for the hosts in the second round.

The final in Paris got off to an exciting start, when both teams scored inside the first seven minutes, Pal Titkos cancelling out Gino Colaussi's opener for the Italians. Hungary, though, were finding it difficult to contain Italy's captain and playmaker Giuseppe Meazza, and it was he who provided the pass

Giuseppe Meazza and Gyorgy Sarosi before the 1938 final

for Silvio Piola to restore the Azzurri's lead on the quarter hour mark. Ten minutes before half-time Meazza slotted the ball through to Colaussi, who beat his marker to grab his second goal. To their credit, the Hungarians refused to buckle and reduced the deficit when, following a goalmouth scramble, centre forward Gyorgy Sarosi poked the ball home midway through the second half. Ten minutes from the end, though, Piola ensured the cup would remain in Italy with a powerful drive that whistled into the Hungarian net.

1950, BRAZIL

Appearing at their first World Cup in Brazil in 1950, England travelled to South America with high hopes that a team containing the attacking talents of Stanley Matthews, Tom Finney and Jackie Milburn would justify their tag as joint favourites alongside the hosts. Even the local press were excited by England's participation, with banner headlines proclaiming 'The Kings of Football Have Arrived'.

Following a routine win over Chile in which Blackpool's Stan Mortensen headed England's first ever World Cup goal, Walter Winterbottom's team travelled from Rio de Janeiro to the mining town of Belo Horizonte to play the USA. Facing a side who had twice conceded six goals to Mexico in the qualifiers, England's stars were expected to win handsomely but after missing a host of chances and hitting the woodwork five times, they were beaten 1-0 in one of the tournament's greatest ever shocks. Another 1-0 defeat in their

Uruguay's Schiaffino equalises against Brazil

final match, this time against Spain, left England to ponder a first experience of the World Cup that had been a complete humiliation.

In a one-off experiment, the four group winners all played each other in a final pool, with the cup going to the country taking the most points. After scoring a total of 13 goals in their emphatic defeats of Sweden and Spain, this looked likely to be Brazil, especially as the hosts would only require a draw in their final match against neighbours Uruguay in the Maracana stadium to become world champions.

A Brazilian triumph seemed even more certain when right-winger Friaca gave his side the lead, just two minutes after the half-time break. Uruguay, though, responded with a series of attacks and were rewarded with an equaliser from Juan Alberto Schiaffino. Ten minutes from time the massed ranks of Brazilian fans in the record 199,854 crowd were stunned for a second time when Alcides Ghiggia fired in the winner for the visitors. Brazil had no answer and, after two decades, the World Cup returned to Uruguay.

1954, SWITZERLAND

England travelled to Switzerland with confidence at a low ebb after two shattering defeats at the hands of Hungary in the months before the World Cup. Their squad, though, was an experienced one, with an average age of 29 thanks in part to the presence of Stanley Matthews, still nipping down the wing at the age of 39.

The bizarre format of the tournament, the first to be televised, meant that the two seeded teams in each group would not play each other, only the other two supposedly weaker teams. England, then, avoided a potentially tricky fixture against Italy and instead opened their campaign against Belgium. The match was a thriller, the underdogs coming back from 3-1 down to force extra-time and, eventually, a 4-4 draw. Needing to beat the hosts to progress to the knock-out stage, England won fairly comfortably thanks to goals by the Wolves duo, Jimmy Mullen and Dennis Wilshaw.

England's opponents in the quarter-finals were the holders

An injury to Puskas damaged Hungary's hopes in 1954

Uruguay, who had just trounced Scotland 7-0 in their final group match. Helped by some poor goalkeeping by Birmingham's Gil Merrick, the South Americans ran out 4-2 winners before going down by the same score to the brilliant Hungarians in the semi-finals. Their opponents in the final would be West Germany, who demolished Austria 6-1 in the other semi-final in Basel.

Having previously thrashed the Germans 8-3 in a group game, Hungary were strong favourites to triumph again in Berne and when they took a two-goal lead after just eight minutes the cup seemed destined for Budapest. Within another eight minutes, though, the Germans were level. Handicapped by an injury to their star player, inside forward Ferenc Puskas, Hungary wilted and seven

minutes from time German winger Helmut Rahn struck his second goal of the game to earn his country their first World Cup in dramatic fashion.

1958, SWEDEN

England's preparations for the World Cup in Sweden were put into disarray in February 1958 by the Munich Air Crash, which claimed the lives of eight Manchester United players. Among the victims were three established England internationals – the great Duncan Edwards, striker Tommy Taylor and defender Roger Byrne – who would probably have featured in Walter Winterbottom's team had they survived.

Drawn in a tough group with eventual winners Brazil, Olympic champions the Soviet Union and the formidable Austrians, England's patched up side got off to a reasonable start with a 2-2 draw against a physical Russian outfit. A goalless draw against the talented Brazilians gave England a good chance of progressing, but a third stalemate against an already eliminated Austria meant they would have to meet Russia again in a play-off to decide who would go through to the quarter-finals. Resisting a media campaign to start Manchester United's 20-year-old winger

A teenage Pele plays against Wales in 1958

Bobby Charlton, Winterbottom saw his team go down to a 1-0 defeat and, frustratingly, return home from the competition before both Wales and Northern Ireland.

Both those teams, though, went out in the quarter-finals to end British interest in the tournament. Nothern Ireland were hammered 4-0 by France, while Wales were beaten by Brazil, 17-year-old striking sensation Pele grabbing the only goal. Pele then grabbed a hat-trick as Brazil crushed France 5-2 in one semi-final, while hosts Sweden saw off West Germany in the other.

In the final in Stockholm, Sweden took a surprise lead after just four minutes – but there was to be no shock result. Two goals by their centre forward Vava put Brazil ahead before half-time, and the game was pretty match settled when Pele added a magnificent third ten minutes after the break. Brazil's left-winger Mario Zagallo made it four with 13 minutes left, and although Sweden replied with a second goal there was still time for Pele to round off a resounding victory for the South Americans with a majestic header.

1962, CHILE

With just two defeats in their previous 17 matches, an England team featuring the likes of goal poacher Jimmy Greaves, midfield playmaker Johnny Haynes and a young

Brazil line up in traditional pose at the 1962 finals

press, England responded with an impressive 3-1 defeat of Argentina, Ron Flowers, Bobby Charlton and Greaves getting the goals for Walter Winterbottom's team. A dull 0-0 draw with Bulgaria then clinched England's place in the quarter-final, where they had the misfortune to come up against the holders, Brazil.

Although missing Pele through injury, Brazil predictably proved too strong and ran out 3-1 winners, two of their goals coming from winger Garrincha, whose bandy-legged running style was the legacy of a childhood bout of polio. The other quarter-finals were won by Czechoslovakia, Yugoslavia and hosts Chile, who had earlier beaten Italy in one of the most violent games ever seen at the World Cup. Two Italian players were dismissed by the English referee Ken Aston, although the Chileans were equally to blame for some appalling scenes in a match dubbed 'The Battle of Santiago'.

The Chileans' underhand tactics were again in evidence in the semi-final, which they lost 4-2 to Brazil. Garrincha, who had again netted twice, was kicked throughout, and when he finally retaliated was promptly sent off. It seemed that he would miss the final against Czechoslovakia, who beat Yugoslavia 3-1 in the other semi-final, until FIFA waived his suspension following a personal plea by the Brazilian President.

As in 1958 Brazil conceded the first goal in the final, but they were soon level through Pele's replacement Amarildo. The same player set up Zito for an easy header 20 minutes from time, before Vava ensured the cup would stay in Brazil by adding a third late on.

1966, ENGLAND

Hosting the World Cup for the first time, England went into the tournament as one of the favourites, the expectation of the nation intensified by manager Alf Ramsey's bold prediction that his side would win the competition.

Ramsey's confidence seemed misplaced after England opened their campaign with a disappointing 0-0 draw with Uruguay, but a trademark Bobby Charlton

Alan Ball's World Cup winners medal from 1966

Bobby Moore in their line-up went into the 1962 World Cup in Chile in fine fettle. The confident mood, though, was soon shattered by a defeat to a Hungary side who were not a patch on the 'Magical Magyars' of the 1950s. Written off by the

Bobby Moore receives the World Cup from the Queen

thunderbolt against Mexico finally got the hosts going. A 2-0 victory over the Central Americans was followed by another comfortable win against France, in a match marred by an ugly tackle by Ramsey's midfield enforcer Nobby Stiles.

In the quarter-final, England struggled to break down an uncompromising and sometimes brutal Argentina, even after the first-half dismissal of their captain, Antonio Rattin. Eventually, though, Geoff Hurst headed the winner from a cross by his West Ham team-mate Martin Peters. After the final whistle Ramsey intervened to stop his players swapping shirts with their opponents, before describing the Argentinians as 'animals' in his post-match press conference.

England's semi-final with Portugal, who had recovered from 3-0 down to beat surprise packages North Korea in the previous round, was a more attractive affair. Two goals from Bobby Charlton gave the home team a healthy cushion, and although Portugal star Eusebio scored from the spot late on, England marched on to their first World Cup final.

Their opponents at Wembley were West Germany, conquerors of the Soviet Union in the other semi-final. England got off to a poor start, conceding a sloppy goal to Helmut Haller after 12 minutes. Soon, though, Hurst equalised with a header from Bobby Moore's quickly taken free-kick and then, in the second half, went ahead when Peters slammed home from close range. With the last kick of the game, however, the Germans levelled with a scrappy goal by Wolfgang Weber.

'You've beaten them once... now go out and bloody beat them again!' Ramsey told his players before the start of extra time. And that's precisely what they did. England restored their lead when Hurst struck a fierce shot which bounced down off the crossbar, the referee

ruling that the ball had crossed the line after consulting his linesman. It was Hurst, too, who confirmed his team's triumph in the closing seconds with a rasping drive into the roof of the net, making him the first – and so far, only – player to score a hat-trick in a World Cup final.

1970, MEXICO

Often described as the best finals in the history of the competition, the 1970 tournament in Mexico provided a feast of attacking football – much of it served up by a wonderful Brazilian side featuring a host of legendary names including Pele, Rivelino and Jairzinho.

Brazil's match with holders England was the most keenly anticipated of the group stages, and lived up to expectations despite being played in blisteringly hot temperatures. England's goalkeeper Gordon Banks was in superb form, making a particularly memorable save from Pele's powerful header, but he was eventually beaten when Jairzinho rifled home what proved to be the winning goal. Victories over Romania and Czechoslovakia, though, saw England join Brazil in the quarter-finals.

In a rerun of the 1966 final, England were paired with West Germany. Alf Ramsey's team seemed set for another famous

Carlos Alberto takes the Jules Rimet trophy for keeps

triumph when they swept into a 2-0 lead, but a mistake by goalkeeper Peter Bonetti, deputising for an unwell Banks, allowed Franz Beckenbauer to pull a goal back for the Germans. Ten minutes from time a back header from Uwe Seeler looped over Bonetti to level the scores, before prolific striker Gerd Muller completed a remarkable recovery with a close range finish in extra time.

The Germans' luck, though, ran out in the semi-final when they went down 4-3 to Italy in an extraordinary match which featured no fewer than five goals in extra time. In the other semi-final, Brazil made light work of their neighbours Uruguay, winning 3-1 after another glittering display.

The final in Mexico City was a dazzling spectacle, providing a fitting end to a glorious tournament. Brazil took an early lead when Pele thumped in a header, but the Italians were on level terms before the break after Boninsegna was gifted a goal by the South Americans' erratic defence. There was no stopping Brazil in the second half, however, as Gerson rattled home a long range shot, Jairzinho scored from close range and, finally, Pele stroked a pass into the path of his captain, Carlos Alberto, who blasted in a low piledriver from the edge of the box to round off his country's third World Cup victory in magnificent style.

1974, WEST GERMANY

The 1974 tournament is primarily remembered for some scintillating performances by a Dutch team appearing at their first post-war World Cup. Led by their imperious captain, the great Johan Cruyff, and adopting a fluid system of play dubbed 'Total Football', Holland were simply sensational throughout.

The first round of matches, though, was most notably for the surprise elimination of Italy following a defeat by Poland, conquerors of England in the qualifiers. Another shock saw the hosts West Germany lose 1-0 to their East German neighbours, although both countries had already qualified for the second round.

For the first time, FIFA dispensed with the knock-out format, instead opting for two groups of four teams from which the finalists would emerge. In the event, the last round of games provided semi-finals of sorts, Holland beating a disappointing Brazil side 2-0 to top one group and West Germany defeating Poland thanks to a Gerd Muller goal on a waterlogged pitch in Frankfurt to head the other.

The final in Munich got off to an incredible start when a superb passing move

Johan Neeskens converts Holland's first minute penalty in the '74 final

by the Dutch straight from the kick-off ended with Cruyff being hacked down in the penalty area. England's sole representative at the finals, referee Jack Taylor, pointed to the spot and Johan Neeskens converted the penalty – the fastest ever goal in a World Cup final. Holland continued to dominate the game but their failure to extend their lead proved costly when the Germans equalised through Paul Breitner's penalty after 27 minutes. Worse was to follow for the Dutch, when Muller put his side ahead just before half-time. Holland found no way through the German defence after the break, and the tournament's outstanding team were denied the trophy their breathtaking football deserved.

1978, ARGENTINA

For a while it appeared that the 1978 tournament might not go ahead as planned in Argentina, following the imposition of a military dictatorship in the country. As worldwide protests against the generals' brutal regime gathered momentum there were demands for the finals to be played elsewhere, but FIFA refused to change the venue.

Whatever their political views, the Argentinian public supported their team with a passion rarely seen at previous tournaments, showering their heroes with ticker tape whenever they made their entrance. Despite losing their final group match to Italy, conquerors of England in

the qualifiers, the home side easily progressed into the second round, which

Mario Kempes scores in the World Cup final in 1978

again was split into two pools of four. After picking up a win and a draw in their first two matches, the Argentinians needed to beat Peru by four goals in their last game to pip Brazil for a place in the final. To nobody's surprise, the Peruvians simply folded and were thrashed 6-0, strike partners Mario Kempes and Leopoldo Luque grabbing two goals each. Conspiracy theorists had a field day, suggesting that the Peruvians had either been bribed or that their goalkeeper, the Argentinian-born Ramon Quiroga, had given the hosts a helping hand.

The other final group was made up of four European teams: Austria, Holland, Italy and West Germany. The key match was between Holland and Italy, which the Dutch only needed to draw to reach the final. In the event, they won the game 2-1 despite trailing at half-time.

Roared on by a near-hysterical crowd in Buenos Aires, Argentina took the lead in the final through the prolific Kempes. A late equaliser by the Dutch sent the match into extra time, but the hosts were not to be denied. Inspired by the midfield promptings of little Ossie Ardiles, they added further goals through Kempes and winger Daniel Bertoni to become world champions for the first time.

Trevor Francis helps outwit France back in 1982

1982, SPAIN

After missing out on the two previous tournaments, England qualified for the first 24-team World Cup in unconvincing style. Once there, however, Ron Greenwood's team got off to a perfect start in their opening game against France when midfielder Bryan Robson drilled home after just 27 seconds – at the time, the second fastest goal in the competition's history. England went on to win the match 3-1, and after straightforward victories over Czechoslovakia and Kuwait, topped their group with something to spare.

A tough draw in the second stage saw England paired with old adversaries West Germany and hosts Spain. After a dull 0-0 with the Germans, England needed to beat the Spanish by two goals to reach the semi-finals but were held to another goalless draw. Frustratingly, two excellent chances were spurned by substitutes Kevin Keegan and Trevor Brooking, both making their first appearances of the finals after missing the earlier part of the tournament through injury.

In the first semi-final Italy, who had earlier sneaked through their first round group with three draws, beat Poland thanks to two goals by the tournament's top scorer, Paolo Rossi. Later that evening, an enthralling match between West Germany and France ended in a 3-3 draw after the French had led 3-1 in extra time. For the first time ever at the World Cup a penalty shoot-out settled the outcome, the Germans emerging as the winners.

The first half of the final in Madrid was a tense affair, the best chance falling to the Italians when they were awarded a penalty. Left back Antonio Cabrini, though, wasted the opportunity, sending his kick wide. In the end it mattered little, as Italy dominated after the break and scored three times through Rossi, Marco Tardelli and Alessandro Altobelli. Paul Breitner replied for the Germans, but far too late to prevent Italy claiming their third World Cup.

1986, MEXICO

Initially awarded to Colombia, the venue for the 1986 tournament was later switched for economic reasons to Mexico, who became the first nation to host the competition twice.

After a stress-free qualifying campaign, England

Maradona's 'Hand of God' goal against England

were expected to do well but they got off to a dreadful start, losing their opening match to Portugal and then being held by Morocco. Adding to manager Bobby Robson's woes, he also lost two of his key players, injured skipper Bryan Robson and midfielder Ray Wilkins, suspended after becoming the first England player to be sent off at the finals.

However, the new-look team Robson fielded in the must-win final group game against Poland performed much better, striker Gary Lineker scoring all three goals in a convincing 3-0 win. Another excellent display, and two more Lineker goals, saw off Paraguay in the last 16, setting up a quarter-final with Argentina.

The match in Mexico City hinged on two moments involving Diego Maradona, Argentina's captain and star player. Shortly after the break he flicked the ball into the net with his hand but, despite furious protests from England's players, the goal stood. Minutes later, Maradona dribbled past the entire England defence before planting the ball past goalkeeper Peter Shilton. Golden Boot winner Lineker replied with a late header, but it was not enough to save England.

Maradona scored another magical goal as Argentina breezed past Belgium and into the final. Their opponents were West Germany, conquerors of France in the other semi-final. The South Americans took a two goal lead and appeared to be heading for a comfortable victory until the Germans scored twice in the final quarter hour, both goals coming from corners. There was still enough time left, though, for the brilliant Maradona to settle the game in Argentina's favour, his superb defence-splitting pass setting up midfielder Jorge Burruchaga for the winner.

1990, ITALY

The 1990 tournament in Italy provided some memorable moments but overall was a rather disappointing spectacle, plagued by overly-cautious football which resulted in the lowest goals-per-game average of any World Cup.

From an England perspective, though, the finals were the most exciting since Bobby Moore and co. triumphed in 1966. Nevertheless, Italia '90 started poorly for Bobby Robson's men with a draw against Ireland. Another draw, against a powerful Holland side, was more encouraging,

Tottenham midfielder Paul Gascoigne earning rave reviews for a dynamic performance. Qualification was then achieved with a scrappy win over plucky minnows Egypt, defender Mark Wright scoring the only goal.

Under pressure from his senior players, Robson had switched to a sweeper system and he retained the formation for the last 16 meeting with Belgium. A tense game looked to be heading for penalties until Gascoigne's free-kick was superbly volleyed in by David Platt for the winner. Gazza, as he was now known to everybody, was again outstanding in a nerve-wracking quarter-final against surprise packages Cameroon, which England won 3-2 in extra time, with Gary Lineker firing in the second of two penalties to settle the match.

In the semi-final against West Germany in Turin England fell behind to a cruelly deflected free-kick, but hit back to equalise through Lineker. Extra time brought no further goals, just a booking for a tearful Gazza – which meant he

Gazza before the tears in the semi-final against Germany

would miss the final should England get there. However, to the dismay of 30 million fans watching back home, both Stuart Pearce and Chris Waddle missed in the penalty shoot-out and the Germans went through.

Their opponents in Rome, Argentina, came through a semi-final shoot-out of their own, against Italy. An ugly, bad-tempered final, which saw two Argentinians dismissed, was also decided from the spot, Germany's Andreas Brehme firing home late on to give his country a third world title.

WORLD CUP HISTORY

1994, USA

For the first time in the history of the World Cup the
1994 tournament was held in a nation, the USA, where
football is only a minor sport. Nevertheless, the
American public responded enthusiastically, with the
total attendance of 3.6 million being the highest ever at
the finals so far.

The fans were rewarded with some exciting games in
the opening round, and a number of shock results.
Bulgaria beat Argentina, Saudi Arabia defeated Belgium
while Jack Charlton's Ireland got the better of a
highly-fancied Italy. All those teams went through to
the second round, however, although Argentina did so
without their captain Diego Maradona, who was
sensationally banned from the rest of the tournament
after failing a drugs test.

The South Americans were soon eliminated, losing a
five-goal thriller to Romania in the last 16. Another east
European team, Bulgaria, pulled off an even bigger
surprise in the quarter-final when they came from
behind to beat Germany. The Bulgarians' opponents in
the semi-final were Italy, with Brazil and Sweden
completing the final four. Both games were close, but
neither of the underdogs survived: in Pasadena, the
Swedes were finally undone by a late goal by Brazil's
diminutive striker Romario; while, in New York, the

Bulgarians succumbed to
Italy's pony-tailed talisman
Roberto Baggio, who claimed
both goals in his side's 2-1 win.

*The World Cup came to
Chicago in 1994*

In a repeat of the 1970 final, Italy and Brazil met to
decide the destination of the trophy in Los Angeles.
Despite the array of attacking talent on show, the game
never really got going. Chances were few and far
between and it was no surprise that the tie had to be
settled by penalties. Italy missed two and Brazil one
before Baggio, the undoubted star of the tournament,
blazed his kick high over the bar to gift the South
Americans their fourth World Cup.

1998, FRANCE

The World Cup was revamped for the 1998 tournament
in France, the most important innovations seeing the
number of entrants expanding from 24 to 32 and the
introduction of the 'golden goal' to settle knock-out
matches which went into extra time.

Having missed out on the finals altogether four years
earlier, England were determined to build on their good
showing at Euro '96. Glenn Hoddle's side began with a
comfortable victory over Tunisia in Marseille but then
lost to Romania, falling to a last-minute winner by

Zinedine Zidane after scoring in the 1998 final

opponent who had fouled him. A man short, England hung on bravely through extra time but eventually lost out on penalties after misses by midfielders Paul Ince and David Batty.

Argentina's World Cup ended in the next round when they lost to Holland, who in turn went out in a semi-final shoot-out to Brazil. The South Americans' opponents in the final were France, who came through their semi-final against surprise packages Croatia thanks to two goals by defender Lilian Thuram.

Brazil's preparations for the final in Paris were thrown into turmoil when star striker Ronaldo suffered a convulsive fit shortly before kick off. Although he played, Ronaldo understandably looked a shadow of his normal self and France won the match convincingly, two headers by their playmaker Zinedine Zidane settling the outcome before Emmanuel Petit added an extra gloss to the hosts' victory with a third goal in injury time.

Chelsea's Dan Petrescu after 18-year-old striker Michael Owen had come off the bench to level the scores. Needing to beat Colombia to be sure of progressing, Darren Anderton and David Beckham came up with the goals to keep England in the tournament.

In the last 16 meeting with Argentina in St. Etienne both sides netted from the spot in the early stages, before Owen put England ahead with a brilliant individual goal. However, the South Americans levelled the scores before half-time and then took the initiative when Beckham was sent off for a petulant kick at an

2002, JAPAN AND SOUTH KOREA

The first World Cup to be held in Asia, the 2002 tournament in Japan and South Korea was attended by hordes of friendly, enthusiastic supporters from the host nations. The local fans were repaid with consistently excellent

David Beckham converts a penalty against Argentina

displays by their own countries, who were among a number of less fancied teams to spring some major surprises.

The main shock in the group stage was the elimination of holders France, after defeats by Senegal and Denmark. Portugal, too, fell by the wayside, following a 1-0 loss to South Korea in the final round of games. There was an upset, too, in England's group where Argentina failed to qualify, the key result being the South Americans' 1-0 defeat to Sven Goran Eriksson's men, England skipper David Beckham smashing home the only goal from the penalty spot. The Three Lions then had little difficulty in disposing of Denmark in the last 16, Rio Ferdinand, Michael Owen and Emile Heskey all featuring on the scoresheet in a 3-0 win.

England's good form continued in the quarter-final against Brazil, Owen giving his side the lead before Rivaldo equalised on the stroke of half-time. In the second half Ronaldinho scored a flukey winner – floating a free-kick over David Seaman's head from fully 40 yards – before being sent off. England, though, failed to make the extra man count and tamely slipped out of the competition.

Both the semi-finals were decided by a single goal: Brazil accounting for Turkey and Germany finally seeing off South Korea, who had amazed even their own fans by knocking out Italy and Spain in the previous rounds. In the first ever meeting between two titans of the World Cup, Brazil's gap-toothed striker Ronaldo proved to be the difference between the teams, grabbing both goals as his side won 2-0 to claim an unprecedented fifth World Cup title.

2006, GERMANY

An unwritten rule of the World Cup states that the winners virtually always come from the continent where the tournament is played. The 2006 finals in Germany took that rule a step further with all four semi-finalists hailing from Europe – this first such clean sweep since 1982.

Among the European sides of whom great things were expected were Sven Goran Eriksson's England. Drawn in an easy-looking group and with a squad of players dubbed 'the golden generation', the Three Lions were viewed as genuine title contenders. They made painfully hard work, though, of their opening fixtures, only beating Paraguay with the help of an own goal and taking more than 80 minutes to break the deadlock against minnows Trinidad and Tobago before running

Fabio Cannavaro lifts the World Cup in Berlin

out 2-0 winners. After two laboured performances, England then played much better against bogey side Sweden, but were held to a draw after defensive lapses allowed the Scandinavians to cancel out a superb volley from Joe Cole and a Steven Gerrard header. Nonetheless, the point from the match was sufficient for England to top the group.

In the last 16, Ecuador provided the opposition in Stuttgart. Once more, England were unconvincing, surviving a number of scares before skipper David Beckham's cleverly curled free-kick proved decisive. With Michael Owen sidelined by injury, Eriksson adopted a cautious strategy against Portugal in the quarter-final, employing Wayne Rooney as a lone striker. The game turned out to be a cagey affair, the key moment arriving just after the hour when Rooney was sent off for stamping on Ricardo Carvalho. Down to ten men, England hung on grimly through extra-time before the match was eventually settled by penalties. As every England fan must have feared, the old shoot-out hoodoo struck again as Frank Lampard, Steven Gerrard and Jamie Carragher all missed before Cristiano Ronaldo confidently slotted home Portugal's winner.

The Portuguese, though, were not so fortunate in the semi-final against France in Munich, going out to a Zinedine Zidane spot-kick. The other semi-final between Italy and Germany in Dortmund, meanwhile, appeared all set to go to penalties until the hosts were undone by two goals in the final minutes of extra time.

The final in Berlin got off to a spectacular start when France were awarded a controversial penalty after just seven minutes. Zidane, cool as ever, chipped his shot in off the crossbar to give his side the lead, but Italy levelled soon afterwards through Marco Materazzi's firm header from a corner. Both sides missed chances to win the match before Zidane was sent off in extra time for head butting Materazzi in the chest in an off-the-ball incident. Italy failed to take advantage of their numerical superiority in the remaining 10 minutes and, as in 1994, the final was decided by the lottery of penalties. The fall guy on this occasion was France's David Trezeguet, whose shot smacked against the bar, allowing Fabio Grosso the chance to clinch the trophy with his side's final spot-kick. Showing no sign of nerves, the left back swept the ball high into the corner of the net and Italy were world champions for a fourth time.

WORLD CUP

RECORDS

TEAM RECORDS

• The most successful country in the history of the World Cup are Brazil, who have won the competition a record five times – in 1958, 1962, 1970, 1994 and 2002.

• **Current holders Italy are Europe's leading nation with four wins, closely followed by three-time winners Germany. South American neighbours Argentina and Uruguay have both won the competition twice, the Uruguayans emerging victorious when the pair met in the first ever World Cup Final in Montevideo in 1930. The only other countries to claim the trophy are England and France, who took advantage of their host nation status to win the competition in 1966 and 1998 respectively.**

• Including both Japan and South Korea, who were joint hosts for the 2002 edition, the World Cup has been staged in 15 different countries. South Africa, the first hosts from the African continent, will make it 16 when the tournament kicks off this summer.

• **The first nation to stage the tournament twice were Mexico (in 1970 and 1986), while Italy (1934 and 1990), France (1938 and 1998) and Germany (1974 and 2006) have also played the role of hosts on two occasions. Interestingly, all seven winners of the competition have triumphed on home soil once except for Brazil, who were denied by Uruguay in the 1950 final in Rio de Janeiro.**

• Brazil are the only country to have played at all 18 tournaments, and will stretch their record to 19 in South Africa. Along with Germany, the South Americans have played in a record seven finals. The same two nations share the record for the most games played at

Brazilian hands lift the World Cup for a record fifth time in 2002

the finals, with 92 each. Brazil, though, are out in front when it comes to total wins (64) and total goals scored (201, including a few pretty decent ones from the likes of Pele, Zico and Kaka).

• **Hungary hold the record for the most goals scored in a single tournament, banging in 27 in just five games at the 1954 finals in Switzerland. Even this impressive tally, though, was not quite enough for the 'Magical Magyars' to lift the trophy as they lost 3-2 in the final against West Germany, a team they had annihilated 8-3 earlier in the tournament.**

• Hungary also hold the record for the biggest ever victory at the finals, demolishing El Salvador 10-1 at the 1982 tournament in Spain. That, though, was a reasonably close encounter compared to the biggest win in qualifying, Australia's 31-0 massacre of American Samoa in 2001, a game in which Aussie striker Archie Thompson smashed in a record 13 goals.

• **Switzerland are the only country not to concede a single goal at the finals, keeping clean sheets in all four of their games at the 2006 tournament before being eliminated in the last 16 by Ukraine in a penalty shoot-out.**

INDIVIDUAL RECORDS

• The legendary Pele is the only player in World Cup history to have been presented with three winners' medals. The Brazilian striker enjoyed his first success as a 17-year-old in 1958 when he scored twice in a 5-2 rout of hosts Sweden in the final, and was a winner again four years later in Chile despite hobbling out of the tournament with a torn leg muscle in the second match. He then made it a hat-trick in 1970, setting a brilliant Brazil side on the road to a convincing 4-1 victory against Italy in the final with a superb header.

• **The leading overall scorer in the World Cup is another famous Brazilian, Ronaldo, who notched 15 goals in total at three tournaments between 1998-2006, including both goals in his side's 2-0 defeat of Germany in the 2002 final. The individual tournament scoring record is held by French striker Just Fontaine scored 13 goals at the 1958 finals in Sweden.**

• England's Geoff Hurst is the only player to score a hat-trick in a World Cup final, finding the net three times against West Germany at Wembley in 1966. His second goal, which gave England a decisive 3-2 lead in extra-time, was the most controversial in World Cup history and German fans still maintain that his shot bounced on the line after striking the crossbar, rather than over it. Naturally, England fans tend to agree with the eagle-eyed Russian linesman who awarded the goal.

• **Just two players have appeared at a record five World Cups: German midfield general Lothar Matthaus (1982-98) and Mexican goalkeeper Antonio Carbajal (1950-66). Matthaus, though, holds the record for games played in the finals, making 25 appearances for his country.**

• The youngest player to appear at the finals is Norman Whiteside, who was just 17 and 41 days when he made his World Cup debut for Northern Ireland against Yugoslavia at the 1982 tournament in Spain. The competition's oldest player, meanwhile, is Cameroon's Roger Milla, who was aged 42 and 39 days when he played against Russia in 1994. It was hardly a day to remember for the veteran striker, though, as Russia won 6-1 with a record five goals coming from the boot of Oleg Salenko.

• **England's Peter Shilton (1982-90) and France's Fabien Barthez (1998-2006) jointly hold the record**

Ronaldo holds the record for the most World Cup goals, as well as the strangest haircut ever seen in the final!

A foul, what us, little Argentina? Maradona pleads innocence in 1994 – a few days before his positive drugs test!

for most clean sheets at the finals, with 10 each. Italy's Walter Zenga, though, holds the record for the most consecutive clean sheets, keeping the ball out of his net for 517 minutes at the 1990 tournament.

• The fastest goal in World Cup history was scored by Hakan Suker, who struck for Turkey after just 11 seconds in the third place play-off against hosts South Korea in 2002. Hungary's Laszlo Kiss scored the fastest hat-trick, finding the net three times in eight minutes after coming on as a sub against El Salvador in 1982.

MISCELLANEOUS RECORDS

• Living up to their reputation for ruthless efficiency, Germany are the most successful side in World Cup shoot-outs, winning all four of their penalty duels including one in 1990 when they beat England in the semi-finals before going on to lift the trophy after a scrappy 1-0 victory over Argentina in the final.

• As most England fans know, the Three Lions have a dreadful record in World Cup shoot-outs, losing all three they have been involved in: against Germany in 1990, Argentina in 1998, and Portugal in 2006. The only other country to lose three shoot-outs are Italy, although they finally managed to win one when they defeated France on penalties in the 2006 final.

• The most unfortunate country in World Cup history are Scotland, who have made eight appearances at the finals without once advancing to the knock-out stages. The Scots, though, were desperately unfortunate to be eliminated on goal difference in 1974, 1978 and 1982.

• The most-played match at the World Cup is between Brazil and Sweden, the two sides having met seven times between 1938-94. Brazil won five of the games, including a 5-2 victory in the 1958 final, while the other two encounters were drawn.

• Argentina have the worst disciplinary record at the finals, having a record 10 players sent off and

88 cautioned (another record) in just 64 games. The earliest red card, meanwhile, was shown to Uruguay hatchetman Jose Batista, who was given his marching orders after just 56 seconds against Scotland in 1986.

• The only player to score for both teams in a World Cup match is Holland's Ernie Brandts, who found the net at both ends in a 2-1 defeat of Italy in 1978.

• Discounting goals scored in shoot-outs, three players have notched a record four penalties at the World Cup: Portugal's Eusebio in 1966, Holland's Rob Rensenbrick in 1978 and Gabriel Batistuta with two for Argentina at both the 1994 and 1998 tournaments.

• The highest scoring match at the finals saw Austria beat hosts Switzerland 7-5 in 1954. The Austrians recovered from 3-0 down to win the match, a feat matched by Portugal when they beat North Korea 5-3 in the quarter-final at Goodison Park in 1966.

• The record attendance for a World Cup match is 199,854 at the 1950 final between Brazil and Uruguay at the Maracana Stadium in Rio de Janeiro. The lowest attendance stands at just 300 for the 1930 clash between Peru and Romania in Montevideo.

• Bora Milutinovic coached a record five countries at the World Cup finals, starting out with Mexico in 1986. The much-travelled Yugoslav then moved on to Costa Rica (1990), USA (1994), Nigeria (1998) and, finally, China (2002).

• The only coach to win the trophy twice is Vittorio Pozzo, with Italy in 1934 and 1938. Just two men have won the competition as both a player and a coach: Brazil's Mario Zagallo (in 1958, 1962 and 1970) and Germany's Franz Beckenbauer (in 1974 and 1990). So far, all the triumphant coaches have been natives of their respective countries... a trend Fabio Capello, for one, will be looking to buck in South Africa.

ENGLAND RECORDS

• Goalkeeper Peter Shilton holds the record for the most England appearances at the World Cup finals, playing in

17 matches between 1982-90. Shilton is also the oldest England player to feature at the tournament, making his last appearance aged 40 and 295 days against hosts Italy in the play-off for third place in 1990.

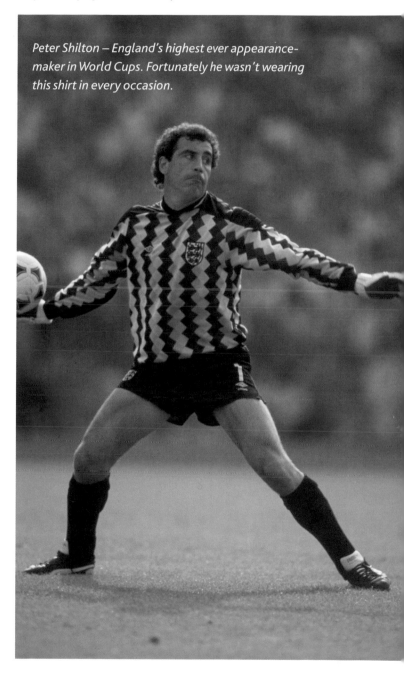

Peter Shilton – England's highest ever appearance-maker in World Cups. Fortunately he wasn't wearing this shirt in every occasion.

• With 10 goals to his name Gary Lineker is England's record scorer at the World Cup. Lineker struck six times at the 1986 tournament – itself a record by an England player – to win the Golden Boot, and then added four more goals at Italia '90 to help his country reach the semi-finals. Along with Geoff Hurst, Lineker is also one of just two England players to score a hat-trick at the finals, grabbing all three of his team's goals in a 3-0 win against Poland in 1986.

Michael Owen skips past the Argentine defence on his way to scoring against Argentina in the 1998 World Cup, aged just 18.

• The only England player to be selected for four World Cups is Bobby Charlton, although he failed to make an appearance at his first tournament in Sweden in 1958. If he features in South Africa, David Beckham will become the first England player to play at four tournaments. Beckham is also the only England player to have scored at three finals, netting against Colombia (1998), Argentina (2002) and Ecuador (2006).

• **England scored a record 11 goals at the 1966 finals, and also enjoyed a record streak of five consecutive wins at the tournament on their way to lifting the Jules Rimet trophy. A sixth consecutive win followed with victory over Romania in England's first match of the 1970 finals in Mexico.**

• Manchester United midfielder Bryan Robson scored the fastest ever England goal – and the third fastest in World Cup history – when he struck after just 27 seconds against France in 1982. England went on to win the match 3-1.

• **The youngest England player to appear at the World Cup is Michael Owen, who was aged 18 and 183 days when he came on as a sub against Tunisia in 1998. Seven days later Owen became England's youngest ever scorer at the finals when he fired home in a 2-1 defeat by Romania.**

• England used a record 19 players at the 1970, 1986 and 1990 tournaments. At the other end of the scale, in an era when substitutes were not permitted, England used just 12 players at the 1962 finals.

• **Three players have captained England at a record 10 World Cup matches: Billy Wright (1950-58), Bobby Moore (1966-70) and David Beckham (2002-06).**

• Just three England players have been sent off at the World Cup: Ray Wilkins (for throwing the ball at the referee against Morocco in 1986); David Beckham (for retaliating after being fouled against Argentina in 1998); and Wayne Rooney (for stamping on an opponent against Portugal in 2006).

MATCH-BY-MATCH SCORECHART

SECOND ROUND

MATCH A
Sat Jun 26 (15.00) Port Elizabeth

1st Group A 2nd Group B

MATCH B
Sun Jun 27 (19.30) Johannesburg SC

1st Group B 2nd Group A

MATCH C
Sat Jun 26 (19.30) Rustenburg

1st Group C 2nd Group D

MATCH D
Sun Jun 27 (15.00) Bloemfontein

1st Group D 2nd Group C

MATCH E
Mon Jun 28 (15.00) Durban

1st Group E 2nd Group F

MATCH F
Tue Jun 29 (15.00) Pretoria

1st Group F 2nd Group E

MATCH G
Mon Jun 28 (19.30) Johannesburg EP

1st Group G 2nd Group H

MATCH H
Tue Jun 29 (19.30) Cape Town

1st Group H 2nd Group G

QUARTER FINALS

QF 1
Fri Jul 2 (15.00) Port Elizabeth

Winner E Winner G

QF 2
Fri Jul 2 (19.30) Johannesburg SC

Winner A Winner C

QF 3
Sat Jul 3 (15.00) Cape Town

Winner B Winner D

QF 4
Sat Jul 3 (19.30) Johannesburg EP

Winner F Winner H